# COUNTRY CHAFF

## by Jerry Easterling

**Binford & Mort**

*Thomas Binford, Publisher*

2536 S.E. Eleventh • Portland, Oregon 97202

*Copyright 1983, Jerry Easterling*

Printed in the United States of America

*Production by Small Farmer's Journal, Inc.*

*Illustrations and cover design by Kristi Gilman*

*Cover Photo by Gerry Lewin*

ISBN 0-8323-0419-0

*To my wife, Jeannie, who makes it all worthwhile.*

# PREFACE

Experiences are the stuff of which life is made. Each is unique, but not all are memorable. Only those that have touched us in a special way linger on in our memories.

The columns in this book are the result of incidents that touched me in that special way. They span the spectrum of human emotion. They reflect the stuff of which life is made.

All are based on true incidents. In most cases, the people involved have not been named, nor have the locales been identified. The columns found here have been separated into seven sections, but no attempt has been made to place them in consecutive or chronological order.

I didn't decide to sit down one day and write a book of columns. In fact, I didn't even decide to write them. John McMillan, present publisher of the *Statesman-Journal* newspaper in Salem, Oregon, suggested the idea while he was the executive editor to whom I reported. I had never written a column, but John, with the instinctual wisdom of a fine editor, thought I might be able to dredge up something out of my rural past that would interest readers.

I was surprised. I was also gratified by the response from readers of the *Statesman-Journal*, in which all of the columns have previously appeared. The sweetest rewards are those we never expect — those that come from people we've never met. To *Statesman-Journal* readers I'm indebted.

# TABLE OF CONTENTS

## REACHING BACK

Remembrance of Grandfather . . . . . . . . . . . . . . . . . . . . . . . . . 1
Haying In A Simpler Time. . . . . . . . . . . . . . . . . . . . . . . . . . . 3
Old Leather . . . . . . . . . . . . . . . . . . . . . . . . . . . . . . . . . . . . 5
Fishing With Grandma . . . . . . . . . . . . . . . . . . . . . . . . . . . . . 7
Simple Things Remembered Best . . . . . . . . . . . . . . . . . . . . . . 9
How Old Tut Bailed Us Out. . . . . . . . . . . . . . . . . . . . . . . . . . 11
Tobacco Chewing Is An Art. . . . . . . . . . . . . . . . . . . . . . . . . . 13
A Special Piece of Americana. . . . . . . . . . . . . . . . . . . . . . . . . 15
A Little Ingenuity Can Be A Dangerous Thing. . . . . . . . . . . . . 17
A Lesson With Punch. . . . . . . . . . . . . . . . . . . . . . . . . . . . . . 19
Opossum Tale Relived . . . . . . . . . . . . . . . . . . . . . . . . . . . . . 21
Child Psychology. . . . . . . . . . . . . . . . . . . . . . . . . . . . . . . . . 23
Going Back For Another Look. . . . . . . . . . . . . . . . . . . . . . . . 25
Missing Links of Life . . . . . . . . . . . . . . . . . . . . . . . . . . . . . . 27
Bridges Take Their Toll . . . . . . . . . . . . . . . . . . . . . . . . . . . . 29
A Gate and Dad's Advice . . . . . . . . . . . . . . . . . . . . . . . . . . . 31
Fence Mending Could Have Produced an Honor Scholar . . . . . . . 33

## A MIXED HARVEST

The Picnic . . . . . . . . . . . . . . . . . . . . . . . . . . . . . . . . . . . . . 35
Old Barns. . . . . . . . . . . . . . . . . . . . . . . . . . . . . . . . . . . . . . 37
The Good Old Days of Chores . . . . . . . . . . . . . . . . . . . . . . . . 39
What Happened To The Thrills?. . . . . . . . . . . . . . . . . . . . . . . 41
Tansy Ragwort Is Coming, Tansy Ragwort Is Coming. . . . . . . . . 43
Despite Troubles, Raising Livestock Is Rewarding . . . . . . . . . . . 45
I Wonder What He Had In Mind? . . . . . . . . . . . . . . . . . . . . . . 47
Pickups Need Breaking In . . . . . . . . . . . . . . . . . . . . . . . . . . . 49
Weekend Farmers . . . . . . . . . . . . . . . . . . . . . . . . . . . . . . . . 51
A Losing Battle With Pigeons. . . . . . . . . . . . . . . . . . . . . . . . . 53
Winter Water . . . . . . . . . . . . . . . . . . . . . . . . . . . . . . . . . . . 55
Farming Is Such Fun . . . . . . . . . . . . . . . . . . . . . . . . . . . . . . 57
Relativity Driven Home . . . . . . . . . . . . . . . . . . . . . . . . . . . . 59
If At Last You Don't Succeed, Give Up . . . . . . . . . . . . . . . . . . 61
Contentment May Be Life's Grandest Reward. . . . . . . . . . . . . . 63
To Look And Never See . . . . . . . . . . . . . . . . . . . . . . . . . . . . 65

## FRIENDS: FEATHERED AND FOUR-LEGGED

The Hawk, A Brave But Untrusting Friend . . . . . . . . . . . . . . . . 67
The Time The Cats Met Their Match . . . . . . . . . . . . . . . . . . . . 69
To A Hog, Freedom Is Something Worth Fighting For . . . . . . . . . 71
Pasquali Met His Match With A Propagandizing Siamese . . . . . . . 73
Animal Relationships . . . . . . . . . . . . . . . . . . . . . . . . . . . . . 75
Somebody Is A Little Mixed-Up . . . . . . . . . . . . . . . . . . . . . . . 77
Bird-Brained? . . . . . . . . . . . . . . . . . . . . . . . . . . . . . . . . . . 79
Memories Of An Elk . . . . . . . . . . . . . . . . . . . . . . . . . . . . . . 81
Wrestling Bear Became A Farce . . . . . . . . . . . . . . . . . . . . . . 83
The Dark Side of the Mind . . . . . . . . . . . . . . . . . . . . . . . . . . 85

## BUYING AND SELLING

A Roundup That Went Wild . . . . . . . . . . . . . . . . . . . . . . . . . 87
Horse Trading . . . . . . . . . . . . . . . . . . . . . . . . . . . . . . . . . . 89
Recollections of One Home's Showpiece . . . . . . . . . . . . . . . . . 91
Dignity Frequents the Oddest Places . . . . . . . . . . . . . . . . . . . 93
Meals For The Memory . . . . . . . . . . . . . . . . . . . . . . . . . . . . 95

## WHO COULD FORGET THEM?

A Lesson In The Color of Hatred . . . . . . . . . . . . . . . . . . . . . . 97
Lifetime Goes On The Auction Block . . . . . . . . . . . . . . . . . . . 99
George, A Man With Old Values Still In Practice . . . . . . . . . . . . 101
Taking It The Way It Comes . . . . . . . . . . . . . . . . . . . . . . . . . 103
The Things That Count . . . . . . . . . . . . . . . . . . . . . . . . . . . . 105
Winners That Lose . . . . . . . . . . . . . . . . . . . . . . . . . . . . . . . 107
Trying To Get A Handle On The Past . . . . . . . . . . . . . . . . . . . 109
An Odd Couple In An Ancient House . . . . . . . . . . . . . . . . . . . 111
Of Strong Fathers And Weak Sons . . . . . . . . . . . . . . . . . . . . 113
Hokey, Who Chose Death As An Answer . . . . . . . . . . . . . . . . 115
Rewards Are Where You Find Them . . . . . . . . . . . . . . . . . . . 117

## A MIXED BAG

What Fun To Weather The Storm . . . . . . . . . . . . . . . . . . . . . . 119
Monotonous Jobs Give Perspective To Life . . . . . . . . . . . . . . . 121
Drawing From Experience . . . . . . . . . . . . . . . . . . . . . . . . . . 123
A Time To Stand And A Time To Fall . . . . . . . . . . . . . . . . . . . 125
Good Times And Bad Times . . . . . . . . . . . . . . . . . . . . . . . . . 127
Indifference Is An Easy Thing To Learn . . . . . . . . . . . . . . . . . 129

## AND THE MOOD CHANGES

March, When The Unexpected Happens . . . . . . . . . . . . . . . . . 131
Spring . . . . . . . . . . . . . . . . . . . . . . . . . . . . . . . . . . . . . . . 133
The Joy Of October . . . . . . . . . . . . . . . . . . . . . . . . . . . . . . 135
Of Thanksgivings, Things Past . . . . . . . . . . . . . . . . . . . . . . . 137
A Witness To The Spirit of Christmas . . . . . . . . . . . . . . . . . . . 139
Time Shares Its Treasures . . . . . . . . . . . . . . . . . . . . . . . . . . 141
Nighttime Magic . . . . . . . . . . . . . . . . . . . . . . . . . . . . . . . . 143

# REACHING BACK

# Remembrance
# of Grandfather

I noticed the small, white oxen yoke standing in the corner of the basement, just as I had a thousand times before. But as I started to leave it caught my eye again, and I went back and dug it out of the accumulation it was almost buried in.

My granddad helped me make that yoke. From a piece of 4 x 6 timber we had sawed it out. Then he had split off some small, thin pieces of oak and patiently showed me how to bend them into bows. Through the center of the yoke he bored a hole and fastened an iron ring to hitch the load to.

"There," he said, as he slowly got to his feet, "it's ready."

Together we ran the two Jersey steer calves I had been given permission to train into the barn, and draped the yoke over their necks. Granddad helped me break them. At first I drove them with long reins attached to halters they wore. Then granddad taught them to come right at the command of "Gee," and left at the command of "Haw."

Still I wasn't satisfied. When you have a yolk of cattle, you should have something for them to pull. So again I turned to granddad, and he helped me to build a sled. On that sled I hauled fodder I cut in the corn field to feed my oxen, and the other calves we had.

It's strange that I can't remember the names of those two Jersey steers. As I looked at that old yoke, I searched my memory, but I guess too much time has passed. I can still see them, though, plodding along in that slow, unhurried pace they set.

1

They stirred granddad's memory. Sometimes in the evening I would sit beside him on the porch as the day closed out, listening to him talk about logging with oxen in Kentucky where he was born. And sometimes he talked about using them on the freight wagons he ran in eastern Kentucky, and on over into West Virginia.

"They aren't fast," he would say. "Not near as fast as mules. But they're steady. On a long pull you can't beat them."

When he worked them in the "log woods," there were usually three or four "span of them" hooked together with a chain fastened to rings in their yokes. When they were on a heavy pull, and the leaders passed over the top of a rise, he said they would pull down so hard on the chain it would force those following to their knees as they topped the rise. I never saw it happen, but I can see those cattle, their eyes becoming wild as they inexorably bowed to weight they could not escape.

My yoke of oxen grew and grew until they had outgrown their yoke. I don't remember when it happened, but the day came when I could no longer fasten the oak bows around their necks. From that day on they were free. I recall thinking as they continued to grow what a powerful team they would have made, even though they were as small as Jerseys are. But by then my fancy had turned to other things.

The years marched on. Granddad and grandma sold their farm and moved to town. Then grandma died, and granddad stayed on alone in that big old white house on the corner. He became lonely, and I remember how he used to beg me to stay a while and talk. "And I'll cook supper," he would say.

But I was always too busy. I thought I had more important things to do. I didn't. I realize that now. And not long after he died I realized that I had never really known him. I could have. He begged me to. But I took what he had to give, and kept on going.

Carefully I put the old yoke back in the corner and climbed the stairs up out of the basement. In a drawer of the filing cabinet I found the note my granddad signed on August 25, 1892 in Mt. Sterling, Kentucky, which was his promise to pay Sylvester Kylton $62 for "1 yoke of cattle."

That's about all I have of Granddad. There should be more. There would have been if I could go back and do it one more time.

# Haying in a Simpler Time

I remember well those days down along the river when everything sought shelter from the sun and nothing stirred, not even a leaf in the heavy hot stillness. Everything, that is, but us, because we were hauling hay. And you've got to make hay while the sun shines. Remember?

I remember. I remember how time piled upon itself, grew static on those long afternoons, seemed never to pass at all until the last load was on its way, waiting till then to sink the sun and turn the day to dusk.

The days were long then, and the nights so short. And sun-slashed mornings that came too soon interrupted sleep so sound. But there wasn't time to drowse. The hayrack's long, springless ride to the field shattered all those lingering dreams and quitting time was a world away.

It seems so long ago. It was a time so different. So many things have happened since. So many things have been done too much and others not enough. There was still a war to be fought then — a World War II — when there were still ideals enough to fight wars for. There was so much to overcome, so many things to change. And youth was on our side then, and the excitement was still to come. Slowly we were riding into the future . . .

Lying back in the hay we'd loaded on the wagon, riding into the barn, hardly feeling the jolts that came rustling up through the hay like rubbery little shocks from explosions far away. And we shaded our faces against the sun to look up at a sky stretched tight as faded denim across our eyes. And the horses quickened pace because they knew it was noon and time to eat.

And how we did. What treats they were, those meals. Fresh peas, swimming with new potatoes in thick cream gravy. Ham, pink as salmon, and as tender. Roast beef the color of mahogany, and grained as fine. Lettuce the green of dollar bills and corn freshly beaded on the cob. And lemon pies. And apple pies. And blackberry. . .

Back in the mind where memories collect I see them still. Back in the mind where things don't age they taste as good as they always did.

Then the haymow: The dark hole, the inferno where hot days concentrated all their heat. And pitching hay in the stifling, dusty gloom, plowing it back from the center where it fell, back along the edges into dusty corners where spiders netted webs. Who knows how hot it got there. No one ever checked because no one ever wanted to. But we knew the devil would have been there if it had been cooler by 20 degrees. Up in the mow you became a salty brine that soon evaporated.

And the big harpoon fork that never ceased to come: the big iron U that lifted the hay off the wagon to the track at the top of the loft. Trying hard to catch up with your breath as the man on the wagon yelled and the horse on the other end of the barn took up the slack and the rope grew taut.

And the harpoon rising slowly, blotting out the light as it climbed in the big mow door — until it reached the end of the track and ran full length of the barn, the hay swinging and swaying in its iron U-shaped arms as it came rolling in. And yelling to the man on the wagon so he could drop the hay — if the rope hadn't tangled up and tripped the fork before it ever got where it was supposed to go.

Forking it back then, working against time, trying to blink the sweat out of your eyes, because the man on the wagon is pulling the harpoon back and you don't want another load dumped on one you haven't got put away.

Then the last load of the day, coming up out of the field in the evening, creaking slowly through the long level shadows, and suddenly it doesn't seem hot any more. And not such a hard day either, not when you're 15 and just being alive and getting through the day is reward enough for living.

That was a good time. I didn't know it then. I wouldn't know it until time and memory had window-dressed it in nostalgia, which so cleverly conceals all the things we want to forget.

# Old Leather

Hanging in our barn is my dad's saddle. He gave it to me before he died. It's an old timer, with a high cantle that keeps you in place. A bucket seat couldn't do a better job. It's a Hercules. A fellow by the name of Davis manufactured it in San Francisco long, long ago.

As I was looking it over the other day, I noticed that the cinch had been lengthened by lacing a piece of leather to one end. When I looked closer, I recognized it. The leather had come from an old boot top, which reminded me that a craft once practiced on a big scale has gone by the board.

When shoes and boots have been well worn today, they are pitched into the trash can. Such was not always the case.

There was a time when they were valued beyond their life expectancy because they were important to the operation of most farms and ranches. At times old leather was almost as essential as baling wire, which has kept more farms operating longer than it takes to total the national debt.

When it came to patching up an old harness, old boot tops were hard to beat. When cut into strips, they could be made to serve most anywhere. They weren't as heavy as harness leather, but if doubled up or tripled, they could be made to work. I've seen harnesses that looked as if they had walked 5,000 miles before they ever found a horse.

And what a boon old leather was for carpenters. Two strips of leather served as well as the fanciest set of hinges. Maybe not quite as well. They did allow doors to sag a little more. And sometimes it was handy to have a crowbar around so you could pry them into place if they were a little too loose, but they served the purpose.

Some people complained about their appearance, but after a while they acquired a quaint charm all their own — if you had a good imagination and didn't care what you said.

Boot tops were of particular value because they could be used as scabbards for tools and holsters, for pistols and revolvers. If they were western boots, they usually had a pretty design stitched into them, and a holster made from them looked as good as one bought out of a store.

They probably wouldn't have received a second glance from Jesse James and Billy the Kid, but that's understandable. They were too busy dodging the hangman's noose to admire good leather work.

The versatility of old leather is truly amazing, when you stop to think about it. I don't know how many times I have seen it used for bearings. When swabbed with grease, it lasts for quite a while before it wears out, and metal begins squealing against metal. I've seen old discs that wore out more boots and shoes than most of us will ever wear.

No one will ever know how many times it was used to keep the engines of old cars hammering along. It was ideal — no, that's not right. It wasn't ideal for use as connecting rod bearings, but that's where a lot of old boot and shoe tops wound up, especially during the Depression when Midwesterners were trying to reach the promised land on the West Coast.

It would stand up pretty well for a while, if the engine wasn't pulled too hard at high speed. But it was only a temporary solution to a major problem. And more than one boot-top mechanic wished he'd saved a little leather to patch the holes in the soles of his shoes after he had walked away from a car with a crankshaft pounded flat.

From the tongues of old boots and shoes, we used to make leather pouches for slingshots. We also cut them into narrow strips that could be used for shoe laces.

But the piece of leather I remember best didn't come from an old boot or shoe. It was a thick strip about an inch wide and three feet long that had once been part of a rein. My dad said it could perform miracles.

I don't know about that, but I know that one licking with it made doing right seem like the logical thing to do. But it wasn't a very smart strap. It didn't have a very long memory. How else do you explain the frequent use it got?

# Fishing with Grandma

When fishing season rolls around, I always think of grandma. I don't think anyone liked to fish better than she did. And I don't think anyone had more of a knack for it. Or more patience. "You got to give 'em time to make up their minds," she used to tell me. "Fish are slow thinkers."

She had learned early. As soon as she was big enough to hold a pole she had started fishing the rivers and streams of Kentucky where she was born and raised. The poles weren't anything to brag about either. Only the rich could afford bamboo rods. Everyone else used willows — or anything that would hold a line.

I don't think she ever fished for trout. And salmon was something you bought in cans when you could afford it. Her specialty was catfish. When she started talking about them, she could really get caught up in the telling. She had pulled out some "whoppers." And if she hadn't caught them, she had seen them after someone else had. One 85 pounder I remember well. It surely must have been a whopper. It weighed more than I did.

I met my grandma in Nebraska, where I was born. Grandad said they'd moved out West because they had four boys that were "so hot-headed they wouldn't have lived to be 21 if they'd stayed in the hills of Eastern Kentucky." One of those hot-heads became my dad.

Grandma couldn't really get too enthused about Nebraska fishing, much as she tried. It wasn't "nothing" compared to fishing in Kentucky, that was for sure. She'd never seen such puny catfish in all her life. And you were just as likely to hook a sucker as anything else, which was the sorriest excuse for a fish that she could think of.

She used to explain those things to me as we fished along a channel that bordered our pasture. And as we sat there with our feet dangling over the bank, she would make my mouth water as she talked about fixing fish "dipped in corn meal batter" to a crunchy, golden brown. That's the way she was going to fix that catfish we were about to catch as the "bobbers" on our lines began dancing in the water.

Most likely they would be bobbing for suckers, those fat, lazy scavengers that lie on the bottom and eat anything that comes along. "Even if it's dead and pugh-trified," she'd say with contempt as she worked hooks out of their little O-shaped mouths and tossed them into the brush.

But I didn't really mind catching suckers. I wouldn't have told her for the world, but I was leery of catfish. When you pulled them in their fins got stiff and sharp as broken glass, and if you weren't careful they'd barb you before you could unhook them.

Once in a while she would give me a hand, but not often. "How you going to fish if you can't even take them off the hook?" she'd ask in a way that made losing a hand sound like a treat.

Our favorite was a big sandpit next to the farm she and grandad owned. It had been dug to furnish gravel for a highway that ran by their place. It was owned by a state representative, who had fenced it tight after it had been stocked with bullheads. It was brushy around the edge, and when I told grandma I had found a place where we could crawl under the high, cyclone fence, her eyes lit up.

We'd go in the evening — in the summer when it was hot and still. That's when the bugs came out and flew low over the dark, flat water. The mosquitos came out then, too. But they came to see how much blood they could draw from us as we hopefully watched our bobbers.

We usually did pretty well when we fished "Old Tom Gass's pond." By switching bait ever so often grandma kept the bullheads coming back for more. And when it was hot and sticky just before a rain we always hauled them in.

Fishing there was a thrill for me. The thought that we were trespassing was never far from the front of my mind, and fear would tingle the back of my neck when she would say: "Shush now, you want to get us caught?"

No, grandma, I don't. And I won't. So come on back and let's go again. It looks like rain and they'll be bitin' tonight. And you know nothing tastes as good as forbidden fish.

8

# Simple Things
# Remembered Best

It stood alone: a small white building surrounded by miles and miles of farmland. It was not ornate. No attempt had been made to conceal its flaws. It had an honest, open appearance. Simplicity was its virtue.

I saw it only once, while visiting relatives. It was on a Sunday morning, and I watched it grow from a tiny white dot on the horizon as we drove toward it. It was the church they attended. Their forefathers had built it. There they gave thanks to the Lord, whose blessings they received with humility.

It was remote, isolated country. Farms and ranches were separated by miles of rough, dusty roads. In the distance, clouds like the one following our car could be seen. They converged slowly upon the little church like dusty spirits coming home. The number of them surprised me. It was more of an occasion than I had expected it to be.

The cars lined up in the worn parking lot, and most of the passengers stretched as they got out. They had been riding a while. A few wore suits. They were either black or navy blue, and most shone with wear. Neckties were knotted uncomfortably around the sunburned necks of all the men, even though some wore overalls.

The women supplied the color, but their dresses didn't flaunt it. The blues were subdued, the pinks pale. The whites were well starched, and browns well pressed. The children were miniature replicas of their parents: the boys dressed like little men, the girls like little women.

The preacher was a young fellow, who knew his people. He spoke their language, and his exuberance aroused smiles and laughter. They liked being close to him. He made them feel good. They waited for him to speak and listened when he did. He had been blessed with that most precious gift: good cheer, which is love of life transmitted.

He didn't live there. He came only on Sundays. From where I don't know, though I remember asking. But it made no difference. He was the attraction. And he wasn't trying to convert anyone. It was a non-denominational congregation.

I don't recall the gist of the sermon, but I remember it was delivered with warmth and vitality. I remember the smiles he accented it with, and the friendly way he looked at his congregation.

There was no stained glass at the windows, and small, white curtains had been drawn back so the sun could stream into the room. It streaked across the worn wooden floor that had been bleached almost white by a thousand scrubbings, and gathered at our feet.

And it seemed right that it should be there. It was as though something beyond us all had stepped in to brighten up the blank, bare walls of that little church. When that occurred to me the old, square-cornered pews seemed softer.

I hadn't been in many churches. We lived quite a ways out of town, and Sundays weren't much different than any other day. The same old chores had to be done, regardless. Cattle had to be fed and barns had to be cleaned. But the Sunday morning I spent in that little white church has stuck with me.

It was all so simple. It seemed that everything had been reduced to the basics, and the basics were care and concern for each other. It made you want to help someone in need, and share in their laughter. It wasn't that special-occasion feeling, either, the kind that vanishes as soon as the occasion is over. It felt natural, like something that would be right for every day.

Though I don't remember the text of the sermon, I was impressed by the lack of "cannots" with which the minister preached. I figured he had broken with conventional religion — or at least the kind I had been exposed to. He made life sound like something it might be possible to enjoy. For that, I've thanked him ever since.

# How Old Tut
# Bailed Us Out

The other morning, after the temperature had sneaked down to 16 during the night, I went out to start the car. And it started, which always surprises me because I'm a throwback to that era when starting a car on a cold morning was an undertaking equal to building the first pyramid.

Cars of the 1920's and '30's were not only phlegmatic on cold mornings, they were downright balky. Engage the starter and the long painful groans they emitted sounded like a 500-pound anvil being dragged over a rock pile against its will.

Since the battery knew from the beginning it was an exercise in futility, it would quickly decide to conserve its energy for more hospitable times. An anemic firefly could have produced more spark.

Sometimes we took a blow torch to the manifold of a recalcitrant engine and tried to warm its cold and steely heart. It didn't often help much, but we felt we had made some progress after the first muffled explosion shot a three-foot streak of flame out of the carburetor. It was good to know that gasoline still burned.

On occasion we built fires under the engines to heat the oil, which congealed in the overnight cold to the consistency of steel wool. But those old cars were vain creatures.

They didn't want to be smoked like a holiday ham, and out of injured pride alone they would refuse to start. It was a matter of principle with them.

When all else failed we would bow to the inevitable. We would go harness "Old Tut," who was 2,200 pounds of black Percheron draft horse. Not until years later did I realize why he got that soulful look in his eyes whenever he saw a car.

Undoubtedly, he remembered all those mornings when he was pressed into service to start one of those mechanical marvels which were supposed to replace him so he could frolic forever in lush green pastures. In later years he assumed the resigned air of one who has been deceived, and expects to be the rest of his life.

His feet would make that cold, crushy sound in the snow as he backed up to the car. Then he would take a long breath, lean into the collar and the tires would break loose from the spot where they were frozen and the car would begin to crunch sullenly along behind him because it rebelled at the indignity of being dragged along behind the very animal it was supposed to replace.

After being towed around and around the yard for awhile, it would begin to gasp and wheeze. Occasionally it would snort between great backfiring convulsions that seemed capable of reducing it to a pile of useless rubble.

But it had no intention of disintegrating. On cold mornings it was just naturally cantankerous. That was basic to its nature. It wouldn't cooperate until it got good and ready.

When it decided it had given us enough trouble, it would erupt with a couple of encouraging coughs. Then it would hit a few times to tease us. After a couple more trips around the yard, it would actually start trying to run in earnest. It would miss and rattle for awhile, before that proud rooster tail of white smoke began rising from the exhaust pipe to let us know we had triumphed once again.

Old Tut would then head wearily for the barn as everyone stood around and exclaimed about how it took only 15 trips around the yard instead of 20 — or 25 which was the record — to get it running, and how it was a pretty good old car after all and getting easier to start all the time.

Cold weather isn't nearly as exciting as it was then. There was always something new to contend with. I enjoyed it — in the same way that I enjoy an impacted wisdom tooth.

# Tobacco Chewing is an Art

There aren't many real tobacco chewers around anymore. I haven't seen any at least. Not the real experts like my Grandad, who could spit through the eye of a needle at 15 feet if he wasn't bucking too much of a head wind.

The wind was a factor, no getting around that. It made him just a wee bit inaccurate. And a bit dangerous at times.

If he happened to be riding up front and all the windows in the car were down it could get just a little juicy in the back seat. If the car was cruising at 50 or 60 and he fired into the slipstream he unconsciously achieved a shotgun effect, which left everything in his wake freckled a liberal brown. He didn't do it on purpose. He just didn't understand the laws of aerodynamics. And he didn't care to learn. He didn't hanker to be an astronaut.

Grandad was a marvel. He didn't spit often. He didn't have to. He swallowed most of the juice. He said it didn't make sense wasting what you'd chewed so hard to produce. And he "chewed a cud" till all the good was gone from it. If he figured there was some left when he went to bed, he laid it on the warming oven of the kitchen stove. When he got up in the morning he grabbed for it before he did his pants.

It must have been beneficial. He never had any stomach trouble and he didn't have any teeth — not even false teeth. But he could tenderize anything enough to get it down, and after that he didn't worry about it. The tobacco juice he swallowed took over from there.

I knew another oldtimer who was quite a chewer in his own right. He was more of a spitter than Grandad was, and a fairly good one too. But his accuracy sometimes left something to be desired. Especially was that true when he got to talking and chewing and spitting all at the same time. You didn't always know where the punctuation was going to land.

Every two years or so he bought a new truck. Since he didn't want to spray tobacco juice all over the side of it by spitting out the window, he set a coffee can on the floorboard so he could fire between his knees.

That worked fine as long as the can was centered, but sometimes the movement of the truck vibrated it off to one side. Old Knute didn't pay much attention to location of the can and he would continue to blaze away with the dark brown results that you can imagine.

I once suggested that he cut a hole in the floorboards so he could fire right on through to the road below. But he wouldn't hear of that. "Cause too much of a draft," he said. "Might blow it back in my face 'n one time through is enough."

I didn't know the old fellow a friend of mine told me about. I wish I had. He was a prospector and a miner, who was still going strong well into his 80's.

In fact, my friend said he got married after he couldn't work a claim anymore just to take his mind off the riches he had never quite discovered a 100 times or more. But marriage, it appeared, was as full of surprises as a hillside full of rattlesnakes. And just about as pleasant.

One day things came to an impasse when his wife wanted to watch a television show at the same time one of his favorites was coming on. In a fit of disgust he went down and ordered a TV of his own. When it was delivered he sat it directly on top of the one his wife watched. Then he shoved his rocking chair up against the wall and sat down. While his wife watched one show, he watched another.

Since he was a tobacco chewer, Ralph said the old prospector set a can beside his chair that was supposed to catch the overflow. But a problem soon arose.

When he'd get caught up in an exciting TV show, he'd blaze away in the general direction of the can without taking aim. And it wasn't long, said Ralph, till the wall next to his chair had turned a rich, dark chocolaty brown.

That in itself wasn't bad, but when the paper began peeling off the wall it began looking a little strange. But there was one nice thing about it: the old prospector didn't have to empty his can very often.

Chewing tobacco is an art. Anyone who has watched an expert exhibit his spitting skills knows what I'm talking about. It's more artistic than Russian ballet. When chewing offers so many possibilities, I wonder why anyone bothers to smoke.

# A Special Piece of Americana

When public dumps became sanitary landfills we lost something. Mountains of Americana went under when the first bulldozer began burying the garbage we turn out in piles that make pyramids look like pimples.

The experts say America's productive capacity has fallen alarmingly, and I guess it has. But I'll bet we reign supreme when it comes to garbage. I don't think any country in the world can throw stuff away faster than we can.

Not until you've visited a dump is it possible to realize how many potions and lotions it takes to beautify, deodorize, de-dandruffize, moisturize and tenderize us all.

I'm not sure there's a correlation between lotions and potions and the sorry state of our industrial production, but there may well be. We had everything smelling so good, and feeling so fine, we didn't realize anything was fishy until we were up to our gills in trade deficits.

I don't know what's going to be done about deficits, but I know we wiped out some mighty fine old institutions when we turned our public dumps into sanitary landfills.

Some people called them "pest grounds," those smoky old pits where discards and disposables were retired. I'm not sure why. Maybe it was because rats increased faster there than Elizabeth Taylor discards disposable husbands.

But they were not bonanzas for rats alone. Many people considered them repositories of great promise. For some they became addictions that couldn't anymore be controlled than an obsessive desire for drugs, or a compulsive craving for booze.

15

I, for one, believe that public dumps were a national treasure. In my estimation, they were comparable to the Grand Canyon and the Redwoods. I wonder why no one thought of that before they started bulldozing them into extinction.

Unless you find dumps intriguing you cannot imagine the thrill — the sheer joy — those blessed souls experienced when they looked out over mountains of refuse mouldering in the sun. A logger surveying a vast forest of virgin timber will know the feeling. And a prospector who discovers the mother lode can share it.

My Aunt Spicy was one of the addicts. She considered a visit to the dump an adventure without equal. If I had been good she would sometimes take me with her. But only if I had been good. A trip to the dump was a reward for exemplary behaviour.

For years I thought it was an acceptable form of recreation. Why it wasn't I'll never know. The odor alone was worth the trip. The fragrance of crushed rose petals was weak and anemic in comparison.

Aunt Spicy was built along stalwart lines, and I can still see her, standing with one hand shading her eyes against a blinding sun as she surveyed a tumbled, jumbled broken-up battlefield of rejected has-beens. Her firm, uncompromising attitude reminded me of a sea captain about to embark upon a voyage to strange and distant lands.

She had an eye for the concealed possibility, the potential yet to be realized. "That old broken wheel over there," she'd say, as her eyes narrowed in shrewd appraisal. "It'll make a good planter with a little work. It'd be nice out back — next to the garden gate. And that over there. . ."

So we'd dig them out. And we always had to dig because everything you wanted was buried beneath something else. That was an unwritten law, an axiom you could depend upon.

Actually, it was a blessing in disguise. Some of our finest discoveries were made while digging something out that had exposed itself just enough to be discovered.

And then they covered them all up. What a crime. Aunt Spicy's nickname described her disposition, and those who came up with that nefarious scheme would have thought twice about putting it into practice if she had been alive.

If they hadn't listened to reason they would have been found ankle deep in the remote corner of some public dump with nothing more than their feet sticking out.

# A Little Ingenuity Can Be a Dangerous Thing

I don't remember what I was doing, but I shouldn't have been. George had taken about all he was going to. I don't blame him. Why we picked on him as we did I'll never know. It seemed he had been created to be a victim. That appears to be the role destiny casts for some.

But suddenly George did something entirely out of character. As he reared up in his seat, he whirled and smacked me hard as he could right in the nose. I wasn't surprised that he had hit me in the nose because it's too big to miss. But I certainly was surprised that he had hit me at all.

I was too stunned to move. And before I could, the teacher moved in to straighten things out, which she was quite capable of doing. I think she was more concerned about George's hand than she was about my nose, which was still echoing like a railroad tunnel. She didn't waste any time consoling those who didn't have it coming.

That was some school. It was a small, one-room affair. Although eight grades were taught there, I don't think more than 15 students were ever going there at once.

The school house sat upon the side of a hill that had been scraped off near the bottom to form a small playground. When the hill was wet it was slick. On the morning George busted me in the nose the hill was wet, which added to my woes.

In my left rear pocket were some matches. They were those big-headed, sulphurous matches. When I slipped and fell as I was heading for the playground at noon I landed on my left pocket and the matches went off. I galloped several smokey circles around the playground because I couldn't get them out. And that just ignited more trouble.

We were forbidden to carry matches and the teacher decided to make an example out of me. When she got through with the paddle she reserved for such occasions, I was pretty well blistered on both rear quarters. But painful as that experience was, it had a positive aspect. It sure made George happy.

For a while another kid and I were janitors at that little school. For $2 a week we were supposed to keep it clean, and see that it was kept warm in the winter. It was heated by a big black heating stove in the corner, which was fired by wood that had to be carried in from a shed outside.

When it was cold, Bob and I had to get there an hour before anyone else because it was a drafty old building that took a long time to heat. Then we hit upon an idea. It was a stroke of pure genius.

In a little while we had piled a stack of rocks up beside the stove. Then we opened the lid and began dropping them into the bed of glowing coals at the bottom of the firebox. Some of them were pretty good sized, but that's the kind we wanted. Once they got hot, we figured they would keep the building warm all night and we wouldn't have to crawl out so early in the morning. We were smugly satisfied as we closed the lid.

Then BOOM! The lid blew open and out shot a shower of cinders, hot coals and ashes that settled lightly all over everything. Somewhere, it appeared, we had miscalculated.

We never did figure out what had happened. But we finally decided that a cavity in one of the rocks had filled with water, which blew it apart when it turned to steam. The tiny flakes of rock we found scattered around the room helped confirm our theory. And the two extra hours we spent cleaning things up confirmed our intention never to do it again.

But our good intentions were not enough. Somehow the teacher found out what had happened and she fired us both, which just goes to prove that a little ingenuity can be a dangerous thing.

# A Lesson with Punch

When they began transporting kids back and forth from school, they deprived them of some valuable "learning experiences," to use a term educators seem to value highly.

I can say with certainty that some of the lessons I learned on the long walk to and from school were much more educational than anything I ever learned in a classroom.

When you were on the road with a half-dozen neighbor kids who didn't want to be there any worse than you did, you just naturally learned a lot of interesting things. And we were definitely on the road.

Most of the schools I attended were at least three miles from home. I guess my folks had heard that walking promotes health, and they wanted to make sure we got our share.

A long walk can be a boring thing if you're not in the mood for it, and we rarely were. For a long time I thought girls had been invented to make them less boring. It's a wonder more women didn't grow up to be man haters the way they were teased and tormented by boys intent upon wringing some excitement out of a three-mile trip to seven hours of classroom confinement.

But there really wasn't much excitement that could be aroused in the morning. The thought of sitting so long in one place blunted the imagination. The effort it took to generate something stimulating usually couldn't be aroused when cramped seats and chalky blackboards were so much in the immediate future.

19

The good things usually happened on the way home from school. A mind that had lain dormant all day despite a teacher's best efforts to revive it, began blooming as soon as the last bell rang. It proved early to me that freedom is the greatest elixir on earth.

Walking home gave us an opportunity to work off the excess energy we had stored up during the day. It was also a time to settle old scores, which a day of inactivity gave us plenty of time to contemplate.

I don't remember what started it, but I have no trouble recalling the fight I had with a kid about my age one bleak afternoon as we began the long walk home. We didn't rush right into it, though.

Even though we might be dying to tear each other apart, we always managed to control our desire until we knew the teacher couldn't see us because she had ways of making fights much more painful than they should have been.

When we decided we were out of her sight we went at each other with a vengeance. We fought along the road. We wrestled back and forth across it. We battled in the ditches, and pounded each other where we could.

We fought until we were exhausted, then walked a ways to get our strength back so we could go at it again. For two miles we did that. The road became a battleground that seemed to go on for a hundred miles. I didn't think it would ever end. We were ready to quit long before it did, but pride kept prodding us on.

By the time it was over, we had wasted a ton of energy. We were battered and bruised, stiff and sore. I distinctly remember how it hurt to get out of bed the next morning. And I have no trouble recalling the lack of sympathy I got when I said I didn't feel like doing chores.

I've often wondered why I remember the fight so vividly, but can't remember the reason for it. If the cause was so easily forgotten, I wonder why we fought.

I've often wondered since if fighting is more important than the cause. If it is, wars are an expression of the same insane urge to hurt and destroy, for which no rational reason can be found.

# Opossum Tale Relived

If it weren't for automobiles, I believe opossums would take over the country. On most any five-mile stretch of Western Oregon highway you'll probably find two or three ironed out on the pavement.

I've tried, but I can't seem to work up much affection for "possums." They're a little too ratty for me. If it weren't for that long scaly tale I probably wouldn't judge them harshly, but that's more than I can handle. And it's certainly more than I want to handle.

But some people consider them a delicacy. I've known a few who thought possum stew was a gustatory experience of the highest caliber. If it isn't of the highest caliber, it's of surely a different caliber.

Near us in Nebraska lived an old Southern couple. They owned a small stone house beside the river where wild grape vines coiled around everything they could reach.

I had a trapline that ran along the river, and once in a while I could see the old man outside. If he wasn't chopping wood, he would be sitting on the chopping block with an old hat settled low on his head, staring off into space.

I tried to avoid him because there was something sinister about that little old stone house and the grape vines that were slowly swallowing it. I was just a kid and my imagination used to run away with itself as I sneaked by the house.

One day the old man yelled at me as I slid down the river bank to keep from being seen. I debated before I decided I had better see what he wanted. I could imagine all sorts of things he might do to make life uncomfortable for me if I didn't.

He was leaning on his axe handle, watching me with faded blue eyes loosely wrapped in folds of thin dry skin. He wanted to know, "Did I ever catch any possums?"

"Once in a while," I told him.

The next time I did, he said he'd like to have one. They're good eating, he told me, with the seriousness most people reserve for politics or religion. Mighty good eatin', yes sir.

He was pleased with the one I brought him. Good and fat, he said. Just right for the pot. He yelled, and a tiny old woman came tottering out of the house with a shawl wrapped around her shoulders. She didn't smile as she peered at me, but she did when she saw the possum.

I was happy I had made them happy and I was relieved to find nothing sinister about them, or the house. But passing by the next day wasn't nearly as exciting. I missed having nothing to fear.

That was short-lived, however. Two days later it turned cold and windy late in the afternoon, and the old man hollered as I trudged along the river bank. He wanted me to come in and warm up for a minute, which was an idea I liked.

Inside it was warm. And musty, and stale smelling. In the kitchen it was gloomy, and my shadow followed me around the walls listlessly, like a faded old ghost.

They were celebrating and they wanted me to join them, since I had provided possum for the occasion. And there on the plate in the center of the table it laid. I felt like I had been trapped, with no prospect of escape.

It wasn't meat on an old plate veiny with tiny black cracks that I saw. In my mind I could still see the possum just as I had given it to the old man. I could see its tail fall limply across the back of his hand when he'd picked it up.

It was pure torture. I chewed on a greasy piece of possum till it was bigger than a football. Then I told them I had to go. When I persisted they sent me on my way with generous thanks for giving them such a fine treat.

The apprehension I had felt about passing the little stone house returned after that. Not because it had regained its sinister appearance. I was afraid they might have another possum they'd insist I share with them.

Checking the trapline became a lot more exciting after that. There's nothing like the threat of a possum feed to keep you on your toes.

# Child Psychology

When Uncle Gyp came to visit, he brought with him what my dad considered some pretty far-fetched ideas about raising kids. Probably because he didn't have any of his own. Uncle Gyp seemed to have all the answers. He put a lot of stock in reason, and firmly believed that all things could be handled reasonably.

He didn't change his mind just because dad disagreed with him. He could have talked two days straight and Uncle Gyp would have remained firm in his belief. With reason, with logic and psychology he beefed up his arguments. From the books, he marched out example after example to demonstrate the rightness of his theory.

"You don't need to punish children," he told dad, "just talk to them. They are reasonable. They will understand."

What he said went right in one of dad's ears and right on out the other. He wasn't buying. What Uncle Gyp said might work where some kids were concerned, but he had a couple of boys who needed something a little more persuasive than a long-winded dialogue about good behavior and its rewards. On that point he was just as adamant as Uncle Gyp was.

I'm not sure when Uncle Gyp's faith began to go. Maybe it was the day I pushed my brother Buggs out of the open door of the hay mow 20 feet up. Or did he push me?

It's immaterial now, but that must have sent a slight shudder of doubt through the foundation on which he based his ideas. Perhaps the day I shot my brother just above the eye with a BB gun was the day he secretly admitted to himself that there were some things the books hadn't touched on.

I'm sure that if he hadn't talked himself into a position he couldn't gracefully abandon, he would have admitted that reason should occasionally be reinforced with stronger measures the day we chained the rear axle of a neighbor's car to the mulberry tree. Even if that didn't the tantrum the neighbor threw should have convinced him that there are few reasonable men in the world.

23

I'm sure his theory trembled with doubt after those incidents. But one was yet to come which reduced it to ruin. And it was ironic because Buggs and I were innocent, a fact Uncle Gyp refused to believe.

He was an avid hunter. He loved to tramp through the fields with his German Shepherd and a .22 automatic rifle. He spent untold hours down along the river hunting rabbits where the brush grew thick.

His rifle was chambered for .22 shorts, which are about a half inch long. And when he was through hunting he often unloaded his rifle and dumped the shells into the pockets of the riding breeches he wore.

Late one afternoon, after he had been tramping through the fields, we were sitting around the living room. I don't remember what Buggs and I were doing. Tormenting our sister Sally, probably, while mother and dad talked to Uncle Gyp.

Suddenly there was a loud bang. At first no one knew what happened, least of all Uncle Gyp who was sitting with ashes all over his face and the broken stem of his pipe sticking out of his mouth. Then it dawned on us.

In the same pocket with the .22 shells Uncle Gyp often carried his pipe. Apparently, he had scooped one up when he pulled his pipe out and hadn't noticed it as he loaded it up for a smoke.

Buggs and I started laughing as we looked for the bowl of his pipe. What a fine trick. I couldn't understand why we hadn't thought of it. Unfortunately, Uncle Gyp thought we had.

With all the innocence that innocence can muster we denied it. But every time he bit down on his sore teeth, Uncle Gyp knew we had deliberately tried to blow his head off. He was a perfect example of a reasonable man who had lost faith in reason.

Not long after that Buggs and I got into another scrape, and with a long, limber willow switch dad chastised the one he thought was guilty.

When he found out he'd whipped the wrong one, he felt bad. But Uncle Gyp didn't share his remorse. By then he was of a different mind about raising kids.

"Don't worry about it," he told dad. "By nightfall he would've had it coming anyway."

# Going Back For Another Look

Once on a Greyhound bus traveling through Eastern Oregon an old man and I shared a seat. After a while he told me he was going back to Tennessee where he had been born and raised.

He hadn't been back for 50 years, he said. For a long time he stared pensively out the window as though he hadn't realized how long he'd been away until he'd said it.

He remembered it all so vividly. That's what surprised me. He told me about the spring water he had drunk as a kid, and how cold it was. And he remembered the streams and creeks he had played in.

But they weren't called creeks and streams in Tennessee, he said, they were called "branches." You could see by the way he frowned that he didn't feel right with a word he hadn't used for so long. But he could still feel the pole that had caught the fish he remembered pulling out of them.

He introduced himself as "Hank." That's all, he said, just Hank. That was all the name a man needed anyway. If he lived a few more years he didn't think he would even need that. By then, he said, everybody was going to be nothing but a number anyway.

As the bus rolled on out over the desert like a schooner at sea, he told me about the hills he had been raised in. And it really did get smokey and blue, he said, and that was the reason they called them the Big Smokies. Feuds were not uncommon there when he was growing up. And sure, hell yes, he'd known lots of moonshiners.

But he remembered best the simple things: the way the sun came up over the mountains, and how white the first snow of winter was.

25

He remembered the birds and the songs they sang. All the things he had enjoyed as a boy came back to him as sharp and clear as "though it was just yesterday."

When we shared that seat, I was in my twenties. And I hadn't thought about that old man for a long time. Not until I went back recently to a place I used to go as a kid.

The small stream that ran there then was shaded by tall fir trees and a tangle of vine maple that grew in close to keep intruders out. If you looked real close you could see faint and lacy footsteps in the soft damp sand where quail had come for water. And sharp cloven-hoofed holes made by deer that had stopped to quench their thirst.

If, on some late afternoon you let yourself quietly down the sloping bank, you might see a grouse disappear as silent as a whiff of smoke among the shadows.

When I went back I didn't expect to find what I had found there on those long afternoons when I had slipped quiet as stealth itself through those trees. But I didn't expect to find what I did on that afternoon not so long ago.

In fact, I had trouble finding it at all. The old ash tree under which I had often sat was gone. There was no vine maple anywhere. And the little stream that had murmured quietly as it rippled in glassy wrinkles over the rocks had lost its voice. Listlessly it followed a concrete channel into a culvert ran over by the road.

Slowly I looked around. It was like being in a dream. I remember thinking: It could have been a figment of your imagination. Perhaps it was. What a strange sensation.

On the hills around were houses that had become homes. Those who lived in them thought everything was as it should be. When that thought occurred to me I realized that I was the intruder.

I had displaced myself in time. It really wasn't the wasteland I thought it was. By some subtle, brain-waved process it had become someone else's dream.

And now I'm thinking about that old man again. I'm wondering how he found things in Tennessee when he arrived. Maybe he took a drink of that spring water and it all came back clear as "yesterday." I hope that's the way it happened.

For the sake of everyone who's looked again, I hope that's true.

# Missing Links of Life

Buzzards aren't designed for beauty. Theirs is not a glamorous life. They don't have the verve or impudence of a blue jay. They are not admired as robins are. And no one ever thinks of them when a hummingbird goes zinging by.

They are in a class by themselves. They are Nature's natural-born undertakers, forever dressed in funereal black. They never laugh. They never smile. Like professional mourners they wait sadly for another's demise. They live high when others die, and never seem to want.

One afternoon in June I watched them loop slowly across the sky toward the wooded hill that stood behind our barn. They were drifting high and lightly on a gentle breeze that smelled of clover. They circled lazily, round and round, as though unwinding the spring that drove them. And lower and lower they began to fly, forsaking altitude for a closer look.

Before they banked sharply and disappeared into the trees, I knew what they had found. Or thought I did — and knew that I had best find out. I didn't want to. It was too fine a day to be reminded of such things. Spring is alive time. It breathes with a warm, fresh breath.

I went slowly up through the trees, among the slanting meadows, the silvery sunlit slashes, and the silence where time was like a

27

peaceful eddy along an endless shore. And I became aware of a strange feeling.

As I slipped quietly through the timber, I began to get tense and my mouth got dry. I noticed I was holding my breath as though I was about to see something I shouldn't. I wasn't scared, but I felt uneasy as if some repulsive secret was about to be revealed to me.

In a small break, where a knot of rough, jagged rocks prevented trees from taking root, the buzzards had found what we had spent two weeks looking for: a calf that had crawled in between two rocks and hadn't been able to get out. With their red wrinkled necks, they looked like evil old men as they ripped and tore at its remains.

I ran out into the clearing, and as I yelled the buzzards flapped around in ponderous disarray as they took off like bloated cargo planes. I don't know what I intended to do, but their gluttony had made me mad. It was obscene. With small rocks I covered what was left of the calf so they couldn't feast on it any more.

I was just a kid then, and after that buzzards went to the top of my list. I declared war on them. When I saw one sitting high in an old snag one day I sneaked around until I was within range, then took careful aim with my .22. It was a long shot, and I heard the slapping sound a bullet makes when it hit, then the buzzard lifted its wings slightly as though to regain its balance. It remained that way for a moment or two before it slowly toppled over backward and plummeted to the ground.

I had scored a victory, but I didn't feel victorious. That uneasy feeling I'd had while sneaking up on the buzzards as they fed on the calf in the clearing had returned. And slowly, like a rising sun, it occurred to me that I had meddled in a plan I had no business meddling in.

I couldn't have explained it at the time. It was more of a feeling than a thought. But as I looked down at that ugly old buzzard, I realized that I had just shot a link out of the unseen chain that connects each to all.

Since then I've seen a lot of links shot out by people in their search for more and more. Nothing is sacred. Nothing remains long if it obstructs their way. So what I want to know is this: what is going to happen when all the links are gone, and there is a chain no more?

# Bridges Take Their Toll

Although they exist for the mundane purpose of getting you from here to there, some bridges are outstanding. And Oregon has some beauties.

The one at Newport arches with the grace of flight as it spans the channel that connects Yaquina Bay to the Pacific. And the one at Waldport soars like a zephyr over Alsea Bay.

And what about covered bridges? In my opinion, they are the aristocrats of bridges. They are genteel, dignified servants that rumbled but never grumbled about the loads they had to bear.

One late spring afternoon I remember walking along a road that led to a neighbor's home where I had been sent for something. I don't remember what I was going after, but I remember the old covered bridge I had to cross. I'll never forget how good it looked when a gusty wind blew up a shower.

As I stood there and listened to the rain fall with a soft, stuttering sound on the roof I felt safe and secure, the way you do when you're around old friends. Covered bridges, I've found, inspire trust.

Bridges can be beautiful, and they can be friendly and trustworthy, but for excitement none compare to swinging bridges. A few I crossed probably shouldn't even be called bridges. They are more like trampolines hanging limply from two loose wires.

One I remember well — very well. It was long and high. Dangling out over the water it looked flimsy as a cobweb built by a spavined spider. It looked too weak and spindly to hold a fly, let alone a human being.

But it would. It would get you to the other side if you didn't mind being held in that loose, sloppy swaying way drunks dancing the Blue Danube hold their partners.

The cables that supported the boardwalk were the handrails. The wires that connected the walkway to the cables served as railings, but they didn't offer much in the way of protection. They were about six feet apart.

In other words, there was plenty of margin for error, which was easy to make in winter when the mossy old boards were wet and slick. I still don't understand how you could slide 25 feet on a board four-feet long, but it was easy on that bridge.

It had a strange effect on your vision. As soon as you looked at it the walkway began rippling lazily, like a slow tango. And the tempo increased as soon as you started across. Or so it seemed.

About halfway out your stomach would usually begin acting in a most peculiar manner. I'm not sure there was a correlation, but it seemed that mine always acted most irresponsibly after a big breakfast of biscuits and gravy topped off with a respectable slab of well greased ham.

Swinging bridges create a strange effect. They're like booze and tobacco: they're addictive. Once they get in your blood you'll wonder why there aren't more swingers than there are.

When I see a swinging bridge, I've got to stop and try it out. Unfortunately, that doesn't happen often anymore. There weren't many to begin with and most of them are gone now.

I still get a thrill when I see one. I know how the economist who finds a cure for inflation is going to feel — if he's not too old to feel by then. But I'm afraid that's going to take longer than it did for swinging bridges to disappear.

I don't know why they affect us as they do. Maybe it's the illusion of danger that attracts us. I was going to suggest that it had something to do with a desire to explore, but I don't think so. Not in my case, anyway.

I'm not interested in the mysteries lurking on the other side. They usually turn out to be an old beer can glinting in the sun anyway. I cross swinging bridges because they are there.

If I could cross swinging bridges before I got to them, I would already be on the other side. I know some that think I am.

# A Gate and Dad's Advice

A flat tire recently reminded me of a wooden gate in Wyoming, which reminded me of my dad. I'm glad he never found out about the gate. I don't think I could have held up under the consequences.

It was another flat tire on a cold, snowy night in Wyoming that brought the gate to mind. If it hadn't been there, I don't know what we would have done. We had no jack, and the truck coming up the hill through the snow wouldn't give us a hand. The driver's words as I jumped on the running board and asked if he had a jack we could use, still ring in my memory today.

"If I stop on this hill," he said, "I'll never get started again. Besides that I got no sand left."

I'm sure he had plenty of sand, which trucks carry in that part of the country to sprinkle in front of the drivers so they won't spin out on those long slick hills. It was piled up at intervals along the highway for trucks to use, and they didn't neglect to use it in bad weather.

I stayed with him almost to the top of the hill, but it did no good. He wasn't going to stop. And didn't. I can't say that I blame him now. But then I did.

I was shivering as I trotted back to the car where Roy was waiting. We had worked together for quite a while and I had never seen him mad. But I saw him get that way.

31

With a fervor passionate and profane he sought to call a catastrophe down upon that truck and driver. I urged him on, but it did no good. They rolled merrily on over the top of the hill and disappeared.

We shivered and looked around. We had to have something we could get under the axle of that old Ford so it could be raised high enough to change tires. That's when we noticed the wooden gate. We wasted no time. Soon there was no more gate but we had a pry-bar we could lift the car with.

The wind was blowing harder, and the snow was sifting along, just inches above the ground in a strange greenish light that seems to go with snowstorms in that part of the country at one o'clock in the morning.

It seemed like hours before we had the car raised and blocked up so we could make the switch. By the time the job was finished, so were we. My fingers were numb and awkward. When he straightened up from tightening the last lug bolt, Roy was shaking so bad he couldn't talk.

After we had pried the car off the blocks we had jammed under the axle, I took one look at the splintered lumber lying there. There was no way it could have been rebuilt as a gate, even if we'd had the inclination. I threw the remnants alongside the barb wire fence. It was a lousy trick, and I hope the rancher noticed the gate was gone before his cattle did. I had run enough stray cattle to know that there were lots of things more pleasant. And in that country they could have gone for miles.

As we drove off I could very distinctly recall the advice my dad had given me a thousand times. "You leave a gate like you find it," he'd say. "If it's open, leave it open. If it's shut, leave it shut."

I don't know what he would have said about leaving no gate at all, but I can well imagine. He was an old cowman, and I'm sure he would have disowned me. He threatened to a number of times for omissions I know he wouldn't have considered half so serious as tearing up a gate.

As I said before, I'm glad I didn't tell him. I would have been hoofing it back to Wyoming with a bunch of 16 foot 2 x 6's over my shoulder to fix that gate if he'd found out. And I'll have to admit that the severity of the punishment would have equalled the seriousness of the crime.

# Fence Mending Could Have Produced an Honor Scholar

When the cows and horses decided there wasn't much to keep them from seeing how green the grass was on the other side, my fine old Grandad used to say it was time to "commence mending fence."

I like to see straight fences, well braced, with wires stretched tight. But Grandad didn't share my view. He didn't consider a fence a thing of beauty. His esthetic tastes ran more to long tall rows of corn that would go "50, 60 bushels to the acre," or fat cattle that could be quickly converted into that long green stuff bankers smile over when mortgages are due. Fences he considered a necessary nuisance, like corns and bunions.

What Grandad did to a fence could hardly be called building. I remember Grandma saying something about him being "out somewhere cobbling up a fence." They did lean somewhat, and they veered a little at times, and in some places they jutted out like a broken elbow. I don't think fences he fixed would have stopped a cow from going where it wanted to, but all the twists and turns he put in them was simply too much for a bovine brain to comprehend.

According to Grandad, there was a reason for mending fences the way he did. "It's easier to keep a crooked fence tight," he'd say as he showered a tired old post with a spray of tobacco juice. I never doubted his word. With all those angles and corners you never had trouble finding a place to take up the slack.

33

For us, fence building was a winter's job. It was a very interesting past-time I can assure you. There is no more rewarding job than trying to dig a post hole in Oregon when it is raining hard and the water table is standing two inches above the ground. I know from experience that nothing will drive you into a murderous rage quicker than trying to dig a hole full of water. If you can do it you've performed a miracle. You'll have no trouble walking across the Mississippi.

But Dad remedied the problem. He made a maul out of oak and wrapped each end with an iron band so it wouldn't split. Then he bored a hole in the center of it, and in that hole he stuck a good stout handle. Then he fastened me or my brother to the end of the handle and instead of digging holes for posts we drove them. The posts, not the holes.

That tough old maul weighed about 16 pounds, and nearly every Saturday while going to high school we could look forward to renewing our acquaintance with it. We built a small platform on which to stand so we could swing down on the post. After swinging that maul awhile, getting on and off that platform was like going up and down Mt. Everest.

I was never fond of school. I devised all kinds of ways to spend as little time in high school as possible. But about 10 o'clock on Saturday mornings I often prayed for a school that would run seven days a week, 365 days a year. Who knows, I might even have been an honor student.

But even fences have their humorous side, if you're on the right side. And for once I was.

After he had set the posts, a neighbor hired a fellow to stretch the woven wire. On woven wire, or "hawg wire" as it is often called, the wires at the bottom are closer together than they are at the top so pigs and lambs can't crawl through.

The fellow he hired had a strong yen for wine, which may have been the reason he hung the fence upside down. But that wasn't the reason he gave.

One morning as he was taking it down so he could put it right-side up, I asked him what had happened. And he said, with obvious disgust, "Some damned fool didn't know which end to put this wire on."

That's understandable. We all get our wires crossed once in awhile.

# A MIXED HARVEST

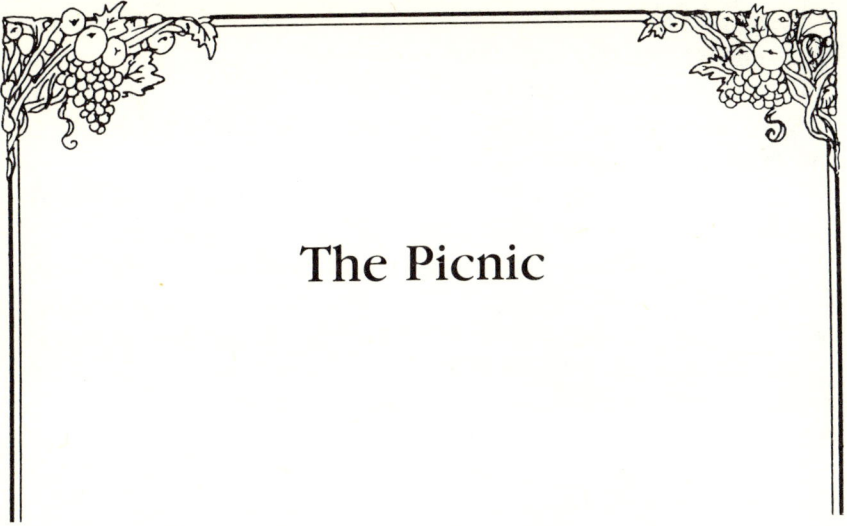

# The Picnic

I was cutting brush and pulling out the rusted wire along a fence line so I could put in a new one. The sun was warm but not hot, and small, puffy, popcorn clouds drifted without rush across a bright blue sky. In a breeze that stirred the leaves, grass rippled like a dark green sea.

As I moved down the fence to another clump of brush I saw our nine-year old daughter, whom we've called Twerp since she was a baby, coming up through the field. She was lugging a big basket, and once in a while I could see her wooly little dog Grover jumping high to see above the grass.

In that basket was our lunch, which she had fixed by herself because she thought I was "probably getting hungry." For us there were sandwiches, cheese and crackers, potato chips, cake and milk. For Grover there was a piece of beef neatly wrapped in cellophane.

We found a shady spot in the grass and sat down to have our "picnic," as she called it. As we ate she told me about the playhouse she and one of her friends were building among some oak trees in the woods on a hill at the back of our place. It was their secret place, she said, but they were having trouble because they didn't have enough chairs.

"You want to see it?" she asked. "It's real nice."

"Yes," I said, "I would like to see it."

"Can we go when we get through with our picnic?"

I wanted to finish clearing out the brush, and normally I would have put her off, the way children are usually put off by adults. But the picnic lunch she had fixed because she was worried that I was "getting hungry," and the way she had talked about her playhouse had given me a glimpse of her world, which I hadn't taken a look at for a long time. I nodded. This was a special moment in her life. And I suddenly realized it was also a special moment in mine.

After she had put everything back in the basket, and tried to feed Grover a cracker he didn't want, we started up through the waist-high grass. As I put my arm around her shoulders, she put hers around my waist, and told me that we were going to her "favorite place." But there was something about the silence among the big fir trees that bothered her. It "kind of scared" her, and she "didn't like to go there alone." I knew what she was talking about. Sometimes I got the feeling that I was being watched by eyes I could not see.

Among a growth of small oak saplings she and her friend had swept the ground clean with an old broom. From the house, they had carried strips of old carpeting, which they had arranged on the "floor." At one point, the ground dipped down, then leveled out again to make a "kind of a sunken living room." With moss they had draped sticks wedged between the trees to form shelves. Old cans had become cookie jars, and . . .

By relying upon the ingenuity that comes naturally to kids, they had created quite a place. And I realized that I was seeing with new awareness a world that we adults so often ignore.

"But daddy," she said, "we need chairs."

Out of an old piece of oak she found on the ground we fashioned something on which they could sit. It doesn't look like a chair, but it is. That is the important thing. There among the oaks they are building one of the finest houses around, but few will ever realize that. I hadn't before, but I do now.

With my arm around her shoulders, and hers around my waist, we went back down through the grass. In a special way our lives had touched that day. Only those who have experienced that special moment will know what I'm talking about. For all others I feel sorry.

# Old Barns

Barns are at their best in the fall, with hay jammed tight against the rafters. They feel good then, when the sky begins to fill with clouds and winter makes its coming known by the sharp, chilled edge it whets on autumn's whisky winds.

To be fully appreciated they need some age, because barns are like people: they reveal their character as they season. It isn't something new barns have. It doesn't come in a can of paint. It can't be nailed on, or hung like a door. If it isn't genuine it isn't there.

It's not something easily described, but if you're a barn addict you can feel it. It's a sense of time. And place. And a feeling of persistence, of steady reliability. And dignified patience, of course.

Barns are masculine, just as houses are feminine. Some may dispute that. Those who beat the drum for equality in all things will probably say that sex has nothing to do with a barn. Or a house. Or with men and women, for that matter. But I stand my ground. Some buildings, such as those that rise like gleaming stilettos stuck into the sky, may be a neuter gender. But that's not what barns are.

An old barn is rough, with drooping shoulders and a tired back that may sag toward the middle. It's tough, rough-cut and splintery. But it's not stingy. It possesses a quality of tired gentleness. Just by looking you can tell that it will never turn anything away. For every stray a place will be found. Inside that scarred old door every creature is welcome. You-all come.

They've got to be built of wood. No other material will do. Nothing reflects time and change the way it does. In time it will crack and brown. It may even warp. But it will persevere. Never will it quit as long as it can hang by the nail that put it there. Its true grain doesn't begin to show until it's been exposed to stress and strain.

Barns are the homage mankind pays to the livestock he domesticates. One is for the other. Without livestock barns are just another building. It takes life to give them warmth. Without purpose barns become empty, hollow shells, just as people do.

In the spring their personalities change. With the hay fed down they seem to open up, to expand. Without something crowding up against the rafters, their roofs rise too high. But winter is past and they have done their duty. As the cattle leave for grass turned green by a friendly sun, old barns fill up with a timeless, restful hush.

Through the cool gloom a fly drones an aimless course, and a thousand tiny, shiny points of dust poise with delicate indecision in a shaft of sunlight squeezing through a crack. A sparrow chitters softly from under the eave, then all is quiet. It's time to relax in the drowsy silence. To doze like tired old men taking the first warm sun of spring.

Then it's summer. And then it's over. And suddenly it's fall again, and mornings come fuzzy with frost. And a silvery stream of fog lingers upon the dark river water like a lover's caress. Soon winter will fill the sky with clouds, and the wind will come hissing around the corners. Old barns seem to squat a little lower then, crouching slightly like tired old fighters. But they've done battle with the elements before. The paint may be gone, but the spirit's still strong.

Inside cattle crowd up against the manger. They are lazy and content. Hay rustles softly as they eat. With patient dignity old barns shelter all those that come to them.

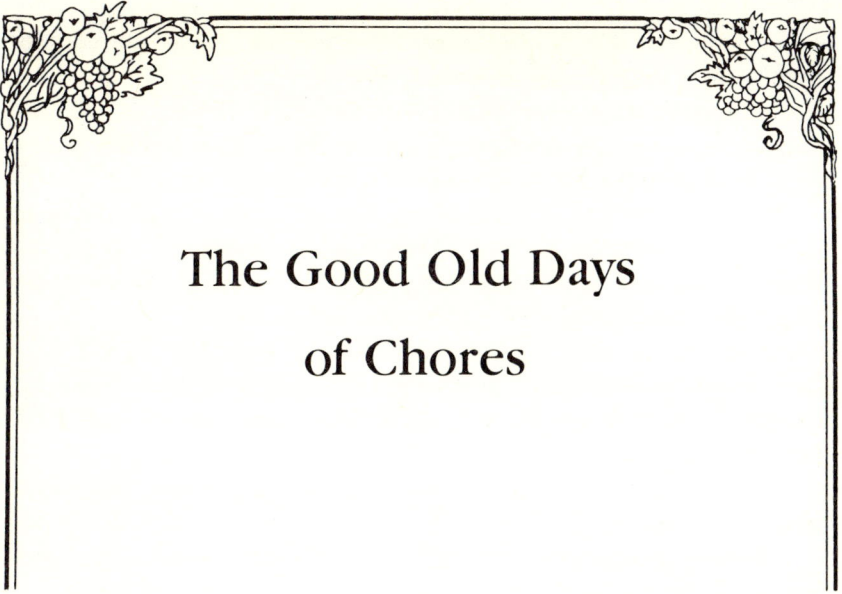

# The Good Old Days

# of Chores

I seem to be going back to the good old days, and I certainly didn't intend to.

Long ago I swore that I would never cut another stick of wood. For a long time I was true to my vow. Then something happened. I think it was called an energy crunch.

I haven't the slightest idea what crunched energy looks like, but I know it takes a lot more than I want to waste on the end of an axe handle.

And it doesn't fit my hands any better than it ever did. In fact, it fits worse. When the axe glanced off a limb the other day and hit my shinbone, it didn't feel any better either. But I'm going to keep at it. And as soon as the Middle East countries run out of oil, I'm going to start peddling wood in downtown Kuwait.

But that isn't the only thing I've gone back to. Long before I decided I would never chop another stick of wood, I vowed I would never milk another cow. But I am. I'm now convinced that every pledge is made to be broken, and not always intentionally.

I didn't induce the black whiteface cow we own to give three times more milk than her calf can drink. But she does. And she's doing it regularly, twice a day. That, at least, is the number of times I'm milking her — once in the morning and once at night.

We've had a war, she and I. She won't stand, so each time I milk, she has to be roped. And each time the loop falls over her head, her determination not to be milked rises higher than Reagan's defense budget. Her eyes grow sullen. When she rolls them back to look at me, it's like looking down the barrel of a 40mm cannon.

At first I thought I could pacify her with sweet talk. I've heard that nearly everything can be accomplished with gentleness and patience. But she knows nothing about the milk of kindness. The kind I get from her isn't high in butterfat, but it sure is rich in resentment.

I've been snubbing her to the trees in our barn lot. I've counted 75 out there, and the ground surrounding each one of them looks like a battlefield.

Some of them have just about been girdled by the rope as she fights her way around in circles. If the calf doesn't get big enough to take her milk pretty soon, we'll have the prettiest grove of dead oak trees anyone's ever seen, all victims of the Great Milky War.

As they say, troubles often come in doubles. And they did. Another old cow we own gave birth to a calf the other day that doesn't weigh more than 40 pounds. And that's not good. She gives more milk per day than it weighs. That means, of course, that she's also got to be milked.

But she's not bad. I can catch her. Sometimes it entails a run from one end of the pasture to the other, which is okay. By the time it's over, we both appreciate a chance to rest.

She doesn't fight when she's being milked. She endures the ordeal while her calf stands off and glares at me. It makes me feel guilty. I never stole from babies before. I didn't cheat either, but I do now. I milk out the easy quarters and make the calf suck the hard ones. But I don't feel too badly about it. The way that calf glares at me, it doesn't deserve one squirt of compassion.

I milk the black white-face first. After warring 30 minutes with her, the old cow in the field is like a pleasant dream. It doesn't sound right — and it doesn't seem right — but milking her is like winning a consolation prize for all the vows I've broken recently. I guess that's what they call serendipity: finding pleasure where you never expected to.

I must be losing my mind.

# What Happened to the Thrills?

Farming sure ain't what it used to be. It's become a high-powered sophisticated operation. If you want to see just how far behind the good old days have fallen, stop by an implement dealer. That new machinery is something else.

Take the modern tractor, for instance. It's a marvel of engineering. It's a wonder they can find anyone smart enough to operate them. I wouldn't crawl into one unless I'd had at least 100 hours of instruction.

I guess they're computerized, too. Everything that can be done electronically is. Soon I suppose they'll have one built into the seat to program the driver as soon as he sits down so he'll know which buttons to push to "get 'er going."

They're nice, there's no getting around that. One grizzled old-timer told me that if he'd had an outhouse half as nice as the cab of a modern tractor, he never would have modernized his house with plumbing. That says a lot for them, as far as I'm concerned.

In the way of comfort, they offer just about everything anyone could want. They represent progress, no doubt about it. But I wonder if they haven't taken some of the fun out of farming.

With those big fancy enclosed cabs they've eliminated the fresh air that is so invigorating during early morning plowing in the spring when the temperature is just a degree or so above freezing.

And it's a shame. There's no better way to wake up. And there's no danger of dozing off again. The chatter of your teeth will keep you wide-eyed and alert.

And what about the good old summer time when temperatures climb to 100 in the shade. How are you going to appreciate it from the inside of a padded cab cooled down to 68 degrees?

You can't. Not until you step out into that rippling, heat-waved inferno and you begin melting down like a pound of lard can you really enjoy it.

And how about the noise? That was part of the thrill. You might not be going more than two miles an hour, but that roaring, red-hot exhaust pipe aroused illusions of power and speed. Of romance, even.

And you'd soon get used to the ringing that lingered on in your ears hours after you had shut down for the day. I'll admit it never sounded quite like Beethoven's Fifth Symphony as played by the New York Philharmonic, but it sounded as good as some of the stuff that's passing for music today.

And where's the dust in modern farming gone? You might see a puff or two drift by the window of a modern tractor cab, but that's no way to appreciate it.

You can't get the feel of farming that way. Not until it fills your eyes to red and runny can you fail to see how it's done. And you'll never know until you can no longer smell the exhaust fumes blowing straight back into your face that your nose is plugged up tight.

Those are some of the things engineers failed to take into consideration when they designed today's tractors. And you really can't get to know the land with the tillage equipment they're designing now.

It used to take a while to go over a field, but today they have plows that will gobble up I don't know how many acres an hour. In three rounds it's all over. It's all over so fast you almost feel like a transient trespassing upon your own fields.

But the real loss, I think is trying to enjoy a cloud of attacking yellow jackets after you've plowed up their nest. From an enclosed cab there's just no way you can appreciate the excitement, the wild confusion, the slappin' 'n cussin' 'n hollerin' that goes on when they begin boring in for revenge. From an enclosed cab you'll never be able to tell by the crooked furrow you left behind how bravely you fought the fight.

Now if you'd been driving horses . . .

But I won't go into that. As Kipling used to say, that's another story, as you can well imagine.

# Tansy Ragwort is Coming, Tansy Ragwort is Coming

Russia will never need declare war on us. If the Big Bear waits long enough we will lose our war in a great forest of tansy ragwort. Mark my word, the day is coming. The Yellow Horde will eventually take us over.

And Russia, I believe, had it figured out years ago. From what I've heard, those tiny little tansy seeds arrived in the United States via a load of grain, or something, shipped in from the U.S.S.R.

They weren't supposed to be there. They should have been detected long before the ship left Russia. The inspectors slipped up. It was an accident, they claimed. But after watching Russia operate, who can say for sure? With her system of espionage, she's sown seeds of dissatisfaction everywhere. And with those first few tansy seeds she began a horticultural revolution that is blooming all over the West, or soon will be.

Any way you say it, any way you spell it — by any name you call it — tansy ragwort is a curse. If you are one of those who enjoys the pretty yellow flowers it makes, you'll never know what I mean. And curses upon you if you do. Those who find beauty in tansy ragwort blossoms could derive a measure of pleasure from a wart upon the nose.

Don't call me a ragwort racist. Let me be the first to say I am. I intend to be one to my dying day. I've taken the vow, solemnly, a thousand times. Everytime I've bent over to pull one of those spangly green demons with the smell I can't describe, I've repeated it to myself. In every way I can, I'll work for the endangerment of their species. I mean, I'm serious.

Unfortunately, what I do, and what I've done, has done so little good. Tansy is winning the battle, on our place at least. It didn't take it by storm. That isn't the way it works. From the Russians it learned a lesson. It moves slowly, with insistent patience, like an aching back. Or, to use another analogy, tansy keeps creeping, creeping like the crud.

And it's deadly. What it does to the livers of horses and cows shouldn't be allowed. If they get enough tansy in their systems, they are goners. And it's not a pleasant way to go. I don't think there is any way to reverse it. By the time the symptoms are noticeable it's too late to do anything about it.

Sheep will eat it. In time, I've heard people say, they will kill it. I don't know about that. But if it's true, they should replace the eagle as the nation's national — what? — not bird, that's for sure — wooly wonders perhaps — and be retired with honor at age five to sweet fields of clover, where they can get rid of the bad taste in their mouths.

I've never tried sheep. Nor the insects that are supposed to have a yen for tansy. I always did it the hard way, the way you cannot win by doing. I was told it did no good to chop it down because another plant will spring from the roots as soon as you turn your back. It had to be pulled, I was told. Pull it and pull it, I was advised, and finally it will go away.

So pull it I did. And found out the hard way that if it is in bloom, or if it is about to bloom, it has to be burned or buried because the pods that were the heart of that pretty little yellow flower will open when dry, and release ten million seeds apiece. And every one of them will take root, and before long all your springtimes will turn into a no-good time.

However, if a few of those seeds fail to germinate, don't worry about them. Those you pulled left some rooty little tendrils deep down in the ground for such contingencies. Before you know it, they will make up for many seeds that went astray. And you'll be so proud of every baby plant they produce.

I think I'll quit right here. Just thinking about it makes my back hurt. When Khruschev said a few years ago that the Russians would bury us, I had no idea they were going to do it with tansy. You've got to watch them all the time.

# Despite Troubles,
# Raising Livestock is Rewarding

The theory of evolution suggests that man descended from animals, though I don't suppose there's one around that would claim us as a relative — not even a distant one.

That could be the reason raising cattle is not all peaches and cream. If they resent being lumped into the same biological class with us, they've found plenty of ways to make us pay.

Take vacations for example. Better still, just try to take a vacation if you're raising cattle. In the good old summertime when everyone else is having fun, you'll be hauling hay so they'll have something to eat when winter comes.

And then, when at last you get a chance to take a few days off, who'll you get to take care of them while you're gone? No one, usually. Who wants to give up all those fun-filled days to make sure a bunch of cows are behaving themselves?

If you're going to raise cattle, chose the variety that's got brains enough to take care of themselves. If you find a breed with IQ's of 100 or more, please let me know.

Chiselling you out of a vacation is not the only thing they excel at. They're even better at going through fences to see how much greener the grass is on the other side. And don't worry, they'll find a way to get there.

You won't have to worry about them coming home, either. Even if the grass isn't as green as they thought it was, they'll keep on looking till they're 100 miles away. With luck, that's where you'll find them after three straight days of searching.

For fouling up their vacation, they may up and get sick just to spite you. And they'll stand around in silent, wordless agony until you try to relieve their misery. Then they'll revive enough to kick you in the head or break your leg. They don't want anyone meddling with their aches and pains.

And nowhere will you find anything as inconsiderate. Bed a barn

45

fresh with straw and see what a bunch of cattle will do to it. But I guess they shouldn't be condemned for that. They've got cousins on the human side of the evolutionary tree that can put them to shame.

When it comes to making a mess, cattle are pikers compared to man. But they're pretty good pikers, and you'd better plan on doing some shoveling when you start raising them. If nothing else, it will keep you in shape.

What they can do to family relations is something no one should have to behold. If you go somewhere in the winter, you'll have to be back by dark to "feed the cows," which makes the rest of the family very happy — especially if they're having fun.

Without the slightest qualm they would trade them all for five more minutes. And they would throw in the ranch for five more minutes after that. They make no bones about it either. By the time you get ready to leave it will be a well advertised fact.

There's something else I've noticed recently. I never noticed it when we were handling a lot of cattle, but since we have only a few I find myself making excuses to keep from hauling them off to the butcher.

Not all of them. Nothing makes me happier than watching one of those wide-eyed, fence-jumping renegades go down the road. But it's a different story with some of the others. I've turned my head so I wouldn't have to watch them go.

You become friends with them. They like you because you like them. When they're calves they'll nuzzle you to let you know how much you're in their thoughts. And they'll do it when they get bigger by trying to knock you down in play.

They learn to trust you. I've watched them walk into a truck because they knew you wouldn't hurt them, turn and look around in wide-eyed alarm when they realize they've been betrayed. That's when you forget about all the trouble they caused.

One time at a slaughterhouse I watched a woman and three of her kids unload a steer they had raised. It didn't want to unload, and as they thought about its fate the kids began to cry. Then the mother began to shed some tears.

By the time they got him unloaded, the steer was the only dry-eyed one around. If they're not getting tangled up in a fence somewhere, they're getting tangled up in your emotions.

# I Wonder What He Had in Mind?

It had rained three, four, or five days straight, and the ground was soggy as an old wet sponge. I guess that's the reason my brother Buggs tried to do what he didn't.

He must have figured he wouldn't have any trouble dozing out a hole for a dead cow he was going to bury. And he must have thought our old crawler tractor had been designed to walk on water. I can find no other explanation for his behavior.

And he's never offered any. When I mentioned it — and I did quite often for a while — he just grinned and clammed up. My misery seemed to give him no end of satisfaction.

It began the moment he dropped the blade and began dozing out that hole. As soon as he had scraped off the tough top layer of sod there wasn't much to support the old "Cat."

I don't think the first pass is the one that got him into trouble. From the looks of things he must have thought he was going to bury an elephant and he made another pass or two to deepen the hole.

By the time he decided it was deep enough, it was. Without further adieu the Cat splashed into the ooze and slowly settled down down down like the tired old machine it was.

I'm assuming it happened that way because I wasn't there. And Buggs wasn't there to explain. After he had sunk the tractor, he took two days off.

I found out what had happened the next morning. When I went looking for the Cat to clean out a big barn where we wintered cattle I couldn't find it. It was strange, I thought, that a five-ton tractor would simply disappear. And it nearly had by the time I discovered it.

It had rained more during the night, and the tractor had settled

47

deeper and deeper into the hole. It looked to me like Buggs had been trying to bury it instead of the cow.

Since the rear end was lighter than the front, the front end had sunk deeper into the hole. It was in so deep water covered half the radiator and part of the fan.

That created a bit of a problem. As soon as I started the engine the fan began churning up a hurricane that soaked the ignition. In a moment the engine started running a little ragged. Then, with a mighty backfire, it shorted out and quit.

I dried off the ignition as best I could, which wasn't easy the way it was raining. And I fished around under water and took the fan belt off to prevent a repeat performance. But it was all in vain. The tractor was high-centered and nothing happened when the tracks began to turn.

With a pickup I hauled some lumber from the barn and began shoving it into the hole while the tractor was running. Usually, it will build up under the tracks enough to give them traction. But it didn't that day.

The lumber simply disappeared. If Buggs had been there I would have sent him in after it. And I would have grinned with glee as the thick, soupy hole devoured him.

After it had swallowed up at least 1,000 board feet of lumber, I decided I was on the wrong track. When I abandoned that project, I got hold of a fellow who had a big truck with a winch on the front.

The pasture was solid enough on higher ground for it to maneuver, and he was able to move in close enough to get a line on the tractor. To his truck we hooked two we owned so it wouldn't slide into the hole with the Cat when he tightened the line.

As it was getting dark that evening we got the tractor out. But one of the tracks rolled off as it slithered around in the hole, and it took another hour to loosen the idler and get it back on. And still it rained.

What bothered me most was Buggs' lack of remorse. He didn't seem at all concerned about the trouble he had caused me. In fact, he seemed to be smugly satisfied with the way things had turned out.

I wonder why. You don't suppose it had something to do with the time I rammed his car into that steel bridge? But that was an accident.

# Pickups Need Breaking In

I have it on good authority that some people live their entire lives without ever owning a pickup. I find that not only hard to believe, but unthinkable.

How do they survive? How bereft they must feel when they wake up in the morning and find their driveways cluttered with two or three useless cars.

They aren't fit to haul garbage in. It's most difficult to get a 30 gallon can of trash in the back seat with two or three passengers. If it's a good full can, the stains it'll leave on the upholstery will be much harder to get rid of than the passengers.

And how about livestock? Ever try to haul a calf in the front seat of a car? It can be done, but it's risky. A friend of mine did and lived to regret it.

It was a Holstein bull about a week old. It was too big to stick in a gunny sack, so Hank tied its legs together and laid it on the floorboards. Just in case it managed to get up he tied a rope around its neck and attached it to the steering column.

Naturally, the calf managed to get up. And by the time it got through lunging around it had yanked the steering column askew. It didn't come completely undone, but from that day on it curved gently toward the right. It required extraordinary skill and nimbleness to keep the car on a straight course. But it was, said Hank, a real asset when driving mountainous roads — as long as they curved the way it wanted to go.

A pickup would have solved the problem, and Hank owned one. That was the ironical thing. But it was a showpiece. It shone like polished ebony. The bumpers gleamed like silver, and the wheels flashed like miniature suns all shined up for a good hot summer. After it had been driven, Hank immediately wiped it down with a rag. If it had been a race horse it would have been retired before it ever hit the track.

The bed was a thing to behold. It was spotless. Hank's loving gaze was the heaviest thing it had ever hauled. His wife once said he would have trouble choosing between that pickup and her.

For a moment Hank's face screwed up thoughtfully, then he shook his head. "I don't think it would be any trouble," he said, as he stroked the pickup's glossy hood.

I didn't consider it a pickup. It could have been hanging in an art gallery for all the good it did. Pickups are to be used, not admired. They are the work horses of the automotive line.

But I'll be the first to admit that it's not easy to break in a new pickup. I owned a couple, and I laid awake nights wondering how best to do it. I didn't want to do anything too abrupt, or dramatic. That sometimes gives them a complex.

Overload one in the beginning and it may wind up thinking it's a $60,000 Peterbilt. From then on it's nothing but trouble. It will always be straining its compression, transmission or rear end trying to impress its friends.

I've tried several ways of breaking in new pickups, and all are equally painful. No one likes to see that new, smooth factory paint job begin to go. That first dent feels worse than having a tooth pulled that doesn't hurt.

But putting one in only takes an instant, and it's less painful in the long run. A couple of taps with a sledge hammer will give the wheel wells that old used, abused look and from then on it's smooth sailing.

There is, however, a way to avoid all the misery. Buy an old pickup that has already been beat up. After someone else has done the suffering you can step in and enjoy the rewards.

That's what I keep telling myself when I look at our old pickup. I feel sorry for the person who drove it off the showroom floor. From the looks of it today, he must have suffered pure agony knocking off the new.

I take my hat off to him. I don't think I could have done it. Sometimes when I look at that hunk of tired old iron I wish he hadn't been quite so thorough.

# Weekend Farmers

Western Oregon is the land of weekend farmers. Each afternoon, five days a week, they go home to an acreage in the country after spending eight hours on a job.

It may be 5, 10, 15 or 20 acres. Sometimes more. I don't know how many chose to live that way, but it is a sizeable number. Some will drive the wheels right off a car so they can battle tansy ragwort the year around on a 10-acre plot 50 miles from their job.

And they exert a considerable influence on the price of small, used farming equipment. A tractor that big farmers ignore because it doesn't have enough power, will be snapped up by western Oregonians who spend their weekends digging in the dirt. And the prices they bring is something else.

Inflation has touched everything, but I wonder if anything has inflated as fast as prices on small farm equipment. From personal experience, I know that the price of some small tractors tripled during the last 10 years. They are used, that is for sure, and it's been a long time since some of them rolled off the assembly line. But that makes no difference. Even though they have been around 20 years or more, they still bring from $1,200 to $1,500.

51

At prices like that, it doesn't take long to invest a pretty tidy sum. There is one advantage, however, to buying equipment for farm use: it can be depreciated. Each year, a certain amount can be deducted from gross income for wear and tear. That does not include wear and tear on the operator. No price can be put on that.

Because used equipment is cheaper than new, it is the variety most weekend farmers wind up with. Usually, it is pretty well worn, and a certain amount of ingenuity is required to keep it patched up and running.

I once heard a farmer complain because most of the hay is now baled with twine. He missed the old haywire. Without it, he said, he couldn't hardly keep his equipment going. In fact, he said, it just about put him out of business.

Old equipment can be a headache, there's no doubt about it. It seems that a shaft will decide to twist off just when all the hay is down and big dark rain clouds are piling up on the horizon. Or a gear will let go when the sun is burning hot and the grain is already shattering because it is overripe.

Since baling wire won't fix that shaft, and chewing gum won't stick the teeth back on that gear, it's time for a trip to town. If you're lucky, the old equipment you've been babying along isn't obsolete. If it is, parts won't be available. If they are, they'll probably have to be ordered from Bangor, Maine, which will take at least two weeks.

Tell that to a rain cloud just waiting to unload, and see what happens. Or try to talk the sun into taking a vacation, and see what luck you have.

You'll have more success convincing your cattle that mouldy hay promotes regularity and aids digestion. And if your neighbor is the right kind of guy, maybe you can borrow his flock of old Rhode Island red hens to combine the grain that shattered out on the ground. To pay for the wear and tear on the old girls, you can always split the eggs with him.

# A Losing Battle with Pigeons

Pigeons are my nemesis. They have me whipped, hands down. Had I said no when that first pair flew dripping and bedraggled into our barn loft one cold and windy rainy day I wouldn't be stuck with the mess I am in. But I didn't. Everything, I thought, should have refuge on such a day as that, which proves that sympathy can become a curse.

What that wind-whipped pair of feathery foreigners didn't realize was that it was only a temporary arrangement. When the clouds cleared and the skies turned blue, they were supposed to leave. I guess I didn't spell out the terms of the contract, or they found something in the fine print I overlooked, because they have become permanent guests.

Two wouldn't have been so bad. I could have lived with them. But suddenly they became four, then six, then eight, then twelve... And I thought: "These babies are really prolific."

Then one day it dawned on me that pigeons don't chip their way out of eggs full grown. Despite their apparent ability to multiply overnight, I realized that they too come into the world, small, helpless and hungry. Since I had been such a gracious host, I guess they felt the need to be the same.

So they went out and invited all their relatives to join them. When they discovered there was still room left, they must have whipped off to every little hamlet and city in the Willamette Valley to invite their second cousins, who graciously invited all their shirt-tail relation. From everywhere they came, homing straight as an arrow into our barn.

Although they haven't said so, their refusal to move convinces me that they are grateful for the $700 metal roof we covered the barn with shortly before they moved in. Instead of protecting the hay we were going to store in the loft, it now protects them.

And they have fertilized it so well I'm afraid a bale of hay may take root right there in the loft, which might not be too bad an idea. Growing a crop of hay in the mow has some advantages I hadn't considered. Getting a mowing machine up those steep stairs might present somewhat of a problem, though.

That's ridiculous, but that's the way they've got me thinking. They fly through my sleep. With this recurring dream they haunt me.

I'm standing in the haymow and they are flying about my head, whirling and dipping crazily. Then a big grey fellow, whom I suspect of being the ringleader, settles lightly on my shoulder and coos softly in my ear: "Forevermore. Forevermore." The insolent bugger.

I called it a dream, but it isn't. It's a wing-whistling, feathery nightmare. I grab for that big grey bird, but he spreads his wings and joins the pack whirling 'round my head. Some morning I'll wake up with a throttled alarm clock in my hands.

Nothing fazes them. Cursing and shouting they seem to enjoy. They know that words will never hurt them. Nor will the sticks and stones I throw — wide of the mark. They don't even mind being shot at, as long as I don't come too close — which I haven't. They know it is just a game.

I could seal off the big opening in the front of the barn through which they come and go. I have an aluminum ladder I could reach it with. But the last time I had it stretched out like that, a gust of wind came along and my heart stopped. It felt like it was buckling in the middle, and at that moment I would have given anything for the wings of a dove — or even a pigeon.

Since watching that, they have become even more brazen. Now, when I walk into the barn, I hear them cooing happily: "Forevermore, Forevermore."

I suppose I could build a new barn . . .

# Winter Water

The cold spell we had a while back reminded me how vindictive Mother Nature can be. With her frosty little quirks she causes all sorts of problems.

I think I can safely say that the water pipes I've thawed out would reach from here to Altoona, Penn., if strung end to end. That might even be a record, I'm not sure. I guess I've just been lucky.

But I never thought so when the pipes that filled the tanks where cattle watered plugged with ice. It didn't take much to do it, either. Just let the weatherman suggest that it was going to freeze and they would refuse to run. And that's when cattle really develop a thirst.

When the weather cools off in the fall, they seldom ever want a drink. They go so long without one they could be mistaken for camels. But just let the pipes freeze and see what happens.

They will crowd around a tank frozen solid with ice — one that would take two days in Hades to thaw — and begin to bawl. To hear them, you'd think they had been deprived of water for days before being made to march non-stop across the Sahara Desert.

So you haul water. But you can hardly ever haul enough. In two hours 20 cattle would lower the Columbia River 10 inches. And a frozen water line is all the cue they need to demonstrate their drinking ability.

Next to hauling water for cattle in freezing weather, I can think of only one thing I enjoy less. That's thawing frozen pipes. And well do I remember some of them.

When we built an addition on the barn we decided to run the pipe for the water tank overhead so we wouldn't have to dig a trench to bury it in. We saved a few minutes then, but we later paid.

As soon as the first north wind began to whisper, it would freeze up tight and we'd have to borrow an electric welder from a neighbor to thaw it out. And we had to thaw it in sections because the leads on the welder weren't long enough to reach both ends at once.

There came a day, however, when our efforts were in vain. By the time we'd get one section thawed, the section we had just thawed would be frozen solid again.

After we had spent an hour or so repeating ourselves, the old guy helping me shook his head and said: "This is kinda like wiping your nose on a hoop, ain't it? There's no end to it."

But there was. The next summer we buried that pipe — but not the memories of all those frozen, frigid fingers when it refused to be thawed.

Not long ago I had another experience with a frozen pipe I'd just as soon forget. It supplied water for the house, and when I found out where it was plugged it had already split wide open.

Since it was frozen hard, I didn't turn off the pump. I was going to cut out the broken section and replace it with a new one before I thawed the line. And so back under the house I crawled.

I failed, however, to reckon with whatever you must reckon with under such circumstances. As I was working away, ice suddenly fired out of the pipe I had just cut like bullets from a gun. Right behind it came a stream of ice cold water.

I tried to clamp it off with my hand, but I couldn't. I yelled for someone to turn off the pump but it's quite a ways from the house and it was a while before the pressure eased off.

As I crawled out from under the house, I could well imagine what an Eskimo feels like when his kayak flips over in the Bering Sea.

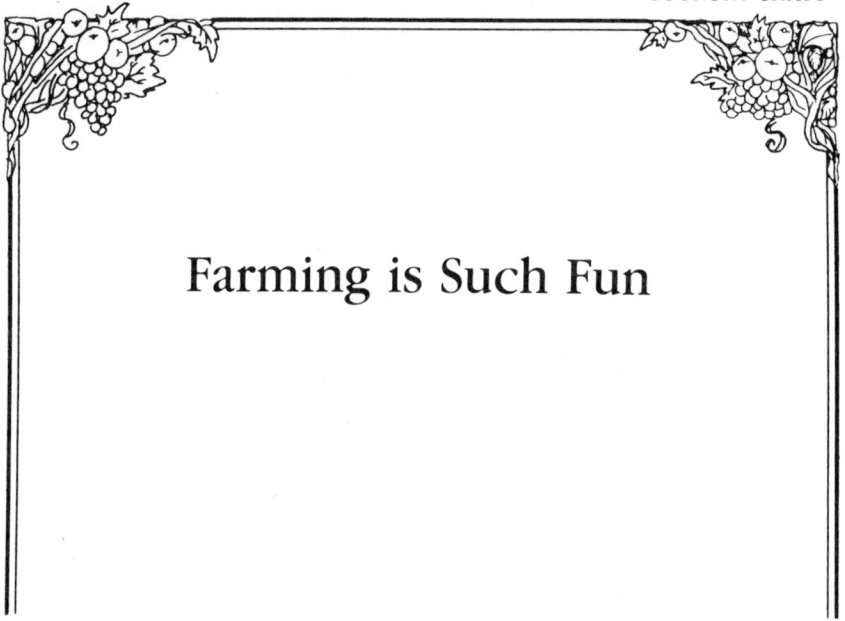

# Farming is Such Fun

Those who keep track of such things tell us that there is a return to the land. It seems that the lights of the city no longer burn with that certain bright promise which has been attracting people for years.

According to statisticians, the exodus from the cities is caused by too much of everything, and not enough of anything. What people are seeking, they tell us, is more room, more fresh air, security, and a chance to live close to the earth. Once acquired, those things will apparently make life worth living again.

What they say about the exodus is true. In the rural areas where it is allowed, subdividers are driving stakes right and left. Anyone with a good arm could play a 60-acre game of horse shoes among the stakes they set. He might sacrifice an occasional shoe to blackberries and Scotch Broom, but with perseverance he could do it.

Those small plots they staked out are in demand. They are being gobbled up faster than worms at a fish farm. Overnight, trailer houses began appearing among fences that zig here and zag there.

Soon a horse is standing in those new-formed fields. Then comes a calf or two, which are good news for the horse. To relieve the boredom, he can run them up and down the fence while visions of Churchill Downs race through his head.

It is plain to see that the horse is enjoying himself. The calves aren't. And most of those bucolic pleasures envisioned by the new rural residents have been conspicuous by their absence. The profits that grew rank as crab grass in his mind before he left the city don't seem to thrive in a countrified atmosphere.

Then comes spring, and the grass greens up. For a couple of months it appears that the paradise he left the city for is his. The horse gets fat and sassy, and the calves begin putting on weight.

But after a few weeks, the grass turns brown and the livestock begins looking over the fence where the grass grows greener. That is when the joys of owning livestock become apparent. With grass hay selling for 50 bucks a ton, and alfalfa going for 70 to 80, the farmer from town learns what an expensive luxury they can be.

That gives pause for sober reflection. The grandeur of the dream has become slightly tarnished, and the new rural resident wonders if there is some way to make his land produce — at least enough to pay the taxes.

Even if there is, it won't be easy. Ask any farmer, one who makes his living from the soil, and he will tell you a few other things about production costs and erratic markets that you don't even want to know.

They come out of the city with high hopes. Many of them talk much of environmental balance and organically grown crops. They are serious. Their expectations are high.

I know one fellow, fresh from Los Angeles, who spent one whole day digging up a big ant hill. Then he moved it so he wouldn't disturb the ants when he planted his garden. That was necessary, he said, if the balance between man and nature was to be maintained.

He worked hard. He built fences and hauled manure to enrich his soil. He toiled away in the evenings after work. He spent his weekend the same way. Then one day he pulled out and turned it over to the ants. He was leaving, he said, because he seemed to be the only element that was out of balance.

# Relativity Driven Home

Someone once said that everything is relative, which turned out to be a fairly accurate statement.

If you have a wart on the end of your nose, you're more fortunate than the person who has two warts on the end of his nose. And neither of you are as fortunate as the person whose nose is wart-less, if a plain, unadorned proboscis is what you want.

Not long ago, as I started up a long hill with a load of cattle on our tired old pickup, I gave some serious thought to the business of relativity. The tiny, thin screechy sound the truck had been making gave me reason to start thinking along those lines.

On the way up the hill, it became louder, more ominous. Before long it began to sound like one piece of metal rubbing another piece of metal with a fair amount of unrestrained exuberance, which is the worst kind when it comes to mechanics.

It was a long hill, and fairly steep. There was only one pullover, which was nearer the top than the bottom. As we labored along, the screechy sound took on a strident note, a good indication that things were going from bad to worse.

Then something let go, and metal started hammering metal. It sounded like King Kong on the loose. I wondered what I was going to do when I got to the pullover — if I ever did.

If the trouble was serious, and it certainly sounded that way, I wondered how I was going to get the cattle home. I thought about driving them, but a 10-mile drive down the middle of a busy highway didn't sound like such a good idea. If one accidentally became the hood ornament for a Lincoln Continental I knew who would pay.

I leaned as far forward over the steering wheel as I could, like a thoroughbred coming down to the wire. I wanted to get as close as I could to the pullover before the old relic quit completely.

We made it. Back down the road 10 miles, the sound of gravel crunching under the tires was the last thing I wanted to hear, but suddenly it was the most beautiful sound I'd heard in years.

The cattle eyed me curiously as I got out and threw a block of wood under one rear tire so the pickup wouldn't try to roll over me when I crawled underneath to see if I could ease its distress. At its age it is entitled to a few complaints, I decided, as I began wriggling around on the gravel, but this is ridiculous.

I was lucky. Instead of some deep, mysterious complication, I found that a rubber cushion that supports the drive line had jumped out of the stirrup that holds it.

With age it had shrunk, and when it worked out the drive line began flopping around in the stirrup like a fish out of water. In relation to a torn-up transmission, I was fortunate. When it comes to relativity that's the kind I like.

It was a hot still day, and everything under the pickup was hotter. From banging against the stirrup the drive line had worked up a real heat. It felt like a streak of fire when I grabbed it the first time. With a pair of old gloves I found under the seat I finally got the rubber cushion back in place, and wedged it there with a couple of big splinters I found by the side of the road.

I crawled back in under the wheel, took a long deep breath, and started the engine. I shifted into gear and let the clutch out in a very slow, exploratory manner. All those disturbing sounds were gone, and we eased timidly back on the highway.

The pickup was still sick, but rigor mortis had been denied. And its condition was such an improvement over its former immobility I could have hugged it.

Since happiness is hugging something, why not? Besides that, it deserved a little affection after the things I had accused it of. In a relative sense it had redeemed itself.

The point of all this, I think, is this: If you must chose between a wart on your nose or a hot drive line, take the wart. In the long run it'll cause you less trouble — relatively speaking.

# It at Last You Don't Succeed, Give Up

The aphids and caterpillars are unhappy this year. So are the mites, the bores, the burrowers and the locusts and the leeches. I didn't plant a garden for them. I didn't actually give up the battle. It was more of a matter of surrendering while I still had something left.

What's left are all the seeds I bought to plant a garden with this spring. At the last minute I decided I wasn't going to be the insect hostess with the mostest any longer. I'm not running a welfare program, although they seem to be in vogue these days. I'm sorry, but I'm not going to be responsible for their health and education and grow them a garden to boot.

It wouldn't have been so bad if just a few had dropped in occasionally for a quick meal before traveling on. I probably could have overlooked that. But that's not the way they operate. They come to stay. And out of insectual (be there such a word?) loyalty they invite all their relatives — and their outlaw in-laws as well.

A chemist for the State Department of Agriculture once told me that thousands of different insect species continually compete for life on this planet we humans so foolishly call our own. I'm sure he was mistaken. There are not thousands, there are millions of those voracious little creatures working round the clock to bring civilization down around our knees.

That may come as a surprise to those who never to themselves have said: "Here I go, a garden fair to grow, hoe, hoe, hoe."

But it's no surprise to those who have hoe hoe hoed blisters on their hands. And it comes as no surprise to those who have put the kink of a crook-neck squash in their backs pulling weeds. They will quickly peg that man from the Department of Agriculture for what he is: a master of understatement.

They can't always be seen, but in my mind I've watched those greedy little gourmands line up along the edge of the garden at planting time like spectators at a football game. And don't think for a minute they don't know what you're doing.

Drop one bean on a hill, listen closely and you'll faintly hear a chorus of tiny voices chanting: "There went a bean to keep us from getting lean." Plant corn and if you listen you shall hear: "There went corn, so don't fret and mourn." "Hey," they'll shout when you plant a beet, "that's really neat."

Even though they can't find a word to rhyme, they'll sing out loud and clear when a potato goes into the ground: "Oh, there's nothing so sweet as a young spud bud."

Don't underestimate them. They're clever. They're smart, persistent little adversaries. They've outsmarted me, year after year. And I can't say that the decision to forego a garden this year was the product of great intellectual insight.

I just finally subscribed to that ancient axiom which states so succinctly: "If at first you don't suceed, try, try again. Then wise up and quit.

I did. I haven't been near our garden spot since. I know there's an angry horde waiting there for me, but it's not fear that keeps me from returning. It's humiliation. By surrendering I lost face. Perhaps I should commit hari-kari on a stalk of wilted celery.

It's begun to prey upon my mind. When I stop and listen I hear them shouting loud as they can:

"There he goes, the wretch so low,
Let's hope he strangles on a tomato he won't grow."

The contemptuous little buggers can't even make a good rhyme, and I'll never plant them another garden — anytime. And maybe they'll lose their minds looking for a juicy sprout they'll never find.

Now they've got me doing it.

# Contentment May be
# Life's Grandest Reward

Josephine was a short, dumpy little woman. She didn't make much of an impression at first, but after a while you began to sense something about her: the serenity that comes with complete happiness.

I met her while we were in the auction business. She lived on a small farm in the remote part of the country where she raised white-face cattle. She wasn't an old hand at it, however.

A few years before, she had moved there from a big city, where she had worked as a bookkeeper. She had made money. She also had accumulated a husband, which she had left because he didn't want any part of country living.

Josephine had a nice place. It was small but well kept. Part of it she irrigated for pasture and hay, which she hired local kids to put up in the summer. She didn't know anything about cattle when she got there, but she learned fast. After she had been burned a couple of times, she knew what to look for. She was a shrewd trader. No one pulled the wool over her eyes the second time.

Raising cattle was something she had always wanted to do. And she loved it, even though she had gotten started late. She was in her late 50's when I met her, but there was a youthful, enthusiastic sparkle in her blue eyes.

Being close to the land gave her more satisfaction than anything she had ever known, she told me one morning as we were getting ready to load a cow she was going to sell.

Not because she was getting rich. She could have done better in the city. But she wouldn't think of going back. Never, she said, had she experienced such peace and contentment.

She felt as though she belonged to something large and mysterious and wonderful. More than once she expressed gratitude for having been strong enough to strike out on her own. For happiness she was willing to take a chance.

Not all who take the chance are so lucky. Harlow wasn't. But he had settled in the country for a different reason. And he tried to settle his wife and family in an environment they resented.

He was a pilot for one of the major airlines. He flew into the Far East when the United States was blowing away its sanity in Vietnam. He was making lots of money, and his schedule allowed him to spend a lot of time on the ranch he had bought in the rolling foothills.

He was also from the city, and he wanted to make a big splash. And he did. For a while he bought cattle like they were going out of style. And all of a sudden winter came and he didn't have nearly enough feed to carry them over. He didn't want to sell any, so he started buying hay. While he was on hand things rocked along fairly well, but they got rough as a cob when he was gone.

His wife didn't like country living — not the kind she was introduced to. And I didn't blame her. She got the short end of the stick when he was flying. There is nothing glamorous about feeding cattle in the mud during a wet and rainy winter, and she got more than her share.

When they failed to get enough to eat, the cattle started breaking out. They began wandering all over the country. Finally someone called the humane society because some were starving. Harlow's dream had become a nightmare. Not long after that he sold out and left.

He came expecting too much. He figured the ranch would make him a lot of money. While it was doing that he expected to harvest a fine stand of happiness. Instead, it produced only frustration and bitterness.

He would have envied Josephine's contentment, but he could never have enjoyed it. His desire to acquire obscured the quiet rewards she reaped. The simple joys she treasured weren't enough for him, and he wound up with none at all.

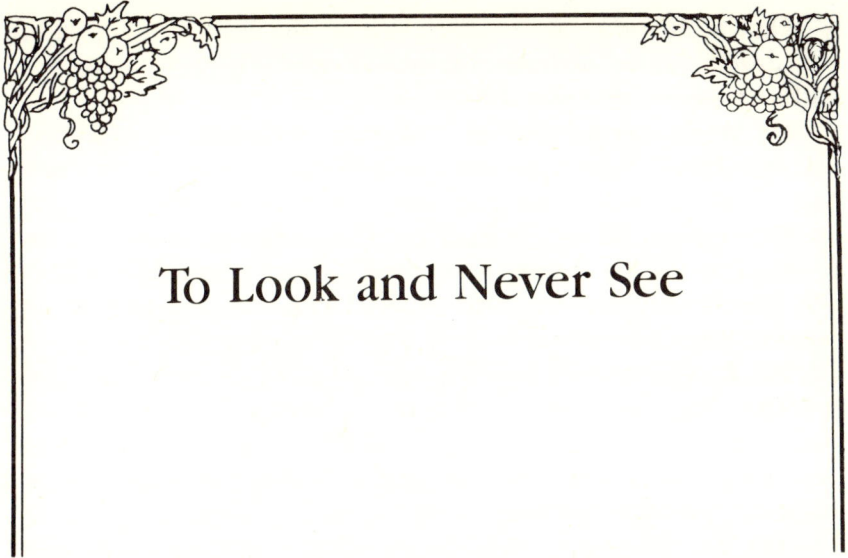

# To Look and Never See

How often do we look and never see. Too often. Far too often. And it's such a sin, to never see . . .

The sun crowding darkness out with light, pushing morning with cautious slowness up into the eastern sky, a giant shiny eye, waiting until all things compose before it looks.

Or the hawk unwinding lazy circles against a pane of pale blue sky, looping high above trees lined up darkly on the hill, a restless phantom racing a silent shadow on the ground.

To look and never see . . .

An oak tree standing so patient and polite, or a stately cone shaped fir of green — or a tired old cottonwood sighing quietly in the breeze.

Or the way grass ripples watery green in a springtime wind, the way it turns brown as bread in late July, then quickly stiffens in autumn's old age and humbly bows to September's silvery frost.

Or swallows back in spring, flitting bluely iridescent in the sun, daubing mud-walled houses to a vacant eave, tiny feathered engines lined like beads upon a wire to rest.

What a sin to look and never see . . .

Cattle coming slowly along the trail in evening stillness when shadows creep quiet as nuns away from all things standing in the sun, where in that hushed and expectant instant all things seem at peace.

Or clouds rising like big dark sails above the mountains in the west, rolling upon each other, great billowy fluffs of steel grey wool getting ready to become a storm.

Or crows cawing through the early morning, insolent black aerialists traveling trails no one can follow in the sky, making noisy fun of all ground-bound creatures whose tracks they can espy.

Or a cobweb strung by a spidery artist between two rusty wires, a net of death that overnight becomes a frosty filigree too delicate, too tremulous in the sun — too touched with beauty to be an instrument of death.

But who has seen it?

The single leaf winding in the autumn breeze, clinging still though dead and dry, to the limb that gave it life, doing an erratic, lifeless dance as it spins away and tumbles lost before the breeze that has blown into winter's first chill wind.

The sun glistening with bluish, blinding brightness off the snow that fell so lightly in the night, where run the tracks of tiny mice, and the wispy tracery of nervous little wrens — a great white silence that becomes a record of all things on the move, but such a fragile record, so soon gone.

The glassy run of water in the sun, and big smooth-washed boulders bald and white, a fish's dreamy drift in a current cold and clear, and a flat, dark ribbon of river curving slowly into a shady, tree-lined bend.

Who has seen . . .

A night chilled clear and a moon so white, and stars flung like a diamond spray above a graceful streamer of fog wrapping like a wreath around the little band of trees standing quiet as Indians on the rise above, and all is tinged with mystery.

Such a loss, to look and never see.

# FRIENDS: FEATHERED
# AND FOUR LEGGED

# The Hawk, a Brave
# but Untrusting Friend

I am his friend. He doesn't know that. Even if he did I'm not sure he would be mine. Hawks don't look to man for companionship. They are much too smart for that. For what he has done to their world, they know he's not to be trusted.

Out in the field, not far from our house, there is a post on which we string electric fence to divide the pasture in the summer. That's his perch. From there he surveys his domain.

And our place is his domain. Part of it, at least, because I don't know how big an area he has staked out. But he knows. In his heart there beats a strong instinctual desire for property of his own.

He's a newcomer. I noticed him the first time in late summer as he came swooping in low over the oak grove of trees that stands between our house and barn. He flew on by, and as he came circling back he shrilled a message to me in that high-pitched chittering voice of his.

I didn't know then, but I know now that he was asking permission to live in our fields, to seek refuge in our trees. In that fierce, yet plaintive cry, the message was clear: he was a drifter looking for a patch of sky in which to unwind his loops, a feathery projectile looking for meadows where mice make tasty targets for his dives.

As I watch him rising tautly on a brisk west wind I envy his freedom, his ability to rise above it all. His grace I admire. And his independence. And the long clean lines of his soaring flight.

But, alas, I've sadly concluded that his freedom is a figment of my imagination. Every day his skies are shrinking and his fields are getting smaller. From his post out in the field he watches in solitary silence the ruination of his world.

He seems to know that this is but a temporary haven. He can sense it. And I can sense his unease when he lifts his wings and circles aimlessly round and round. From the sky he can see the inevitable approaching. He knows by now that what is his today will not be his tomorrow.

From where did he come? When was he crowded too far? What house, or housing project gobbled up the land that had been his to hunt? At what moment in a sad and lonely flight did he decide that it was no use, that he could stay no longer? And when did he climb high into a jet-scarred sky of vapor trails and fly away?

Every day I see him. Every day I watch him watching from his perch out in the field. I know he won't be there long. One day the warning system in his handsome little head will say: "The danger's growing greater. Man is all around. It's time to go again."

There is something grand and tragic about him sitting out there on his post alone. And brave too. And so vulnerable, because he's become a feathery future without a promise. Where tomorrow will he find a place to stay? And after that, where?

One day he will come sailing in over the oak trees and as he lifts on a rising wind he'll call down to me and I'll recognize the sadness in his voice as he says goodbye.

Then he'll be gone.

# The Time the Cats Met Their Match

Unless they were special favorites, the cats around our place stayed in the barn where they were expected to devour rodent population explosions before they happened. They weren't exactly tame. Once in a while you might see one slinking through the shadows like a dusky spirit from a feline underworld.

They were a hardy breed. They could take care of themselves. They could handle just about anything that came along. They were long, lean and rangy. Even big dogs found one encounter with those spitting, hissing whirlwinds sufficient. They didn't go back for seconds. If they went anywhere it was back to where they had come from, mighty fast.

One day a surprising thing happened. A neighbor dropped in and said he wanted to talk. Occasionally, he would rub his eyes and blink as though he had seen something he couldn't quite believe.

Had he been a drinking man, he said he wouldn't have been surprised to see pink elephants tripping across his barn floor. But when he saw grey and white rats — and spotted rats big as cats — scampering around as brazen as could be, and him stone sober, he began to think somebody had loaded his chewing tobacco up with what he didn't know about. Never, he said, as he stared off into the distance, had he seen anything to "beat 'em." He didn't know where they had come from. They were a mystery, sure enough.

He'd tried trapping them, but that hadn't worked. He had shot a few, but that hadn't done much good either. As soon as they found out he was going to be anti-social, they just holed up and refused to come out while he was around. He was at the end of his rope, he said, and that's how come he was there.

They just plain had him buffaloed, and he thought he might be able to slow their increase down if he could borrow a couple of cats. He wondered if we would mind.

He didn't have to borrow the cats, we told him. He could have them. Catching them might be somewhat of a problem though. You just didn't walk over and pick them up like you would old Tabby. If you surprised one you might be within 30 feet, but you didn't surprise them all that often. They could hear a shadow fall.

Since he was desperate, Zeke built a cage out of chicken wire and rigged a door he could trip while hidden behind some hay. Then he put a dish of milk inside the cage and sat down to wait.

Within an hour or so he had trapped two, but it sounded more like a den of pumas when he dropped the trap and those cats discovered they couldn't get out. When he pulled out with them still in the cage he had tied down to the bed of his truck he was grinning from ear to ear.

For three days he said his barn sounded like a jungle. Those big rats fought like tigers, and soon the cats were beginning to show signs of wear and tear. He said "five or six nights of straight tom-catting" couldn't have been any harder on them. He was proud of the way they were holding up. And slowly, he said, they were winning the battle.

Once, to show his appreciation, he fed them a big batch of fresh liver and they responded by stretching out and sleeping 24 hours straight. He was convinced by then that they were super felines, and their behavior upset him. He said it was disappointing to find them acting so much like human beings.

Just about the time the cats had done their job, Zeke found out where the rats had come from. One of his boys, it seemed, had traded some marbles for a pair of tame white rats that had gotten away while he was trying to hide them in the barn so his mother wouldn't know.

When they began consorting amorously with their brethren in the wild, little ones began to appear in various shades of brown and grey and white. Since they were hybrids, they were blessed with size and vigor superior to that of their parents.

There is a moral in this, I think. I think it is this: Don't send your sons to school with marbles in their pockets if you don't want to be invaded by a herd of king-sized, spotted rats.

# To a Hog, Freedom is Worth Fighting for

The snout of a hog is an instrument with an amazing capacity for destruction, and the hogs we were fattening knew how to use them. In no time at all the lot we had fenced them in looked like an Army testing ground for mortars.

We expected that. And we knew they would soon begin working on the fence. We also knew it wouldn't take them long to root their way to freedom. So we decided to take some defensive action. Before they took it into their heads to get out, we decided to ring them.

Hog rings are made of heavy wire bent slightly oblong to form an awkward circle. Between the sharpened ends there is a gap. With a special plier-like tool, the points are squeezed through the rim of a hog's snout. That tenderizes the snout and makes it sore. In theory, rings are supposed to keep hogs from rooting.

It runs into a real job. Each hog has to be caught and held while the ring is being put in. Holding a 70 to 80 pound shoat is like wrestling a warm wad of lard. You're never quite sure whether you've got it, or it's got you. All doubt is erased, however, if one of them bites you.

For a while the rings did what they were intended to. But soon their snouts toughened up, and the hogs were turning the world upside down again. And they can do it. A hundred hogs could have rooted out the Panama Canal in a week. I would have bet on it.

With them back in form again, we knew the fence wouldn't hold them as it was. So we stretched a barbed wire just beneath the netted hog wire. We stretched it just above the ground, as tight as we could. It slowed them up — temporarily.

They were pretty big by then, and they ignored the barbs on the wire we had stretched. It appeared that their sense of feel diminished in direct proportion to their size. And they aren't very sensitive to begin with. While being vaccinated I've seen needles stuck an inch deep into the fleshy part of their necks without them even knowing it. A hog's subcutaneous nerves, a vet once told me, are as far apart as saints and sinners.

Consequently, it wasn't long until they had rooted their way to freedom. And there is nothing they like better than a bed of flowers in a well-kept yard while on the loose. Unfortunately, such forays blossom quickly into something not so lovely as a rose by any other name.

Freedom is pretty heady stuff, and once they had sampled it we couldn't keep them in. Nothing worked. Then a neighbor said he could stop them with an electric fence. That was before electric fences had been perfected, and we didn't know what he had in mind. But we watched closely as he wired things up to the battery of his old Buick, then attached some kind of coil to step up the voltage.

With a sigh of relief we waited for the results. And grinned broadly when the first hog came into contact with that charged wire. It was quite a jolt. It took the curl right out of his tail. He backed off and grunted. And when he charged he went through the wire without even slowing down. With happy oinks of joy the others followed him out.

When Buck saw them coming, he growled and backed up under the car. Then let out a terrified howl and sailed into the car through one open door and out an open window on the other side. As I was looking around for the cause of his distress, I happened to touch the car and let out a howl that put the dog to shame. I had uncovered the mystery.

When the hog broke the fence wire, it had somehow shorted out the car. The tires kept the juice from going directly to the ground, but it went with a jolt through anything that touched the car. Those hogs never got the benefit of it though. They never touched the car. Only Buck and I did that. That must mean something.

# Pasquali Met His Match with a Propagandizing Siamese

I called him Pasquali. He was a fine cat, too. He was big and yellow, with long hair and a stubby little tail. He looked like a bob-cat, which is the reason I took him when a neighbor offered him to me as a kitten.

He was different. He didn't meow much, not even when he was little. He was independent as most cats are, and I think he was pretty much impressed by who he was. He moved with a slow, regal gracefulness, the way tigers in the wild do.

But he wasn't at all wild. Nor was he mean. He'd purr your arm off if you stroked him a couple of times. He was a lot of company, until spring came. Then, with a lusty yowl, he was off to join the pack.

In the early morning hours he would come dragging home, much the worse for wear. The scars he bore were a history of those flaming spring-time nights. As he grew older I think he dreaded their coming. If he hadn't been so determined to honor tom cat tradition I think he would have ignored them altogether. By then he had plenty of progeny to carry on for him. Short-tailed cats were becoming as plentiful in our neck of the woods as tansy ragwort is today. Pasquali could have rested on his laurels had he wanted to, but he had a reputation to uphold.

He was a fighter. A good one. I didn't think there was a cat around who could whip him, but I saw him meet his match. And he lost in a most disgraceful way. Without raising a paw, without baring a claw, he turned and slunk away, which proved to me that propaganda is more effective than a battle royal.

I expected Pasquali to fight when we brought home a pair of Siamese cats. They were intruding upon his domain, and I knew from past experience what he thought of feline intruders. Since he was bigger than the Siamese tom cat, I expected him to establish his authority in short order.

He came marching in from the pasture where he had been hunting in that slow, king-kat swagger of his, and was halfway up the steps of the porch before he noticed the new arrivals.

Slowly his big yellow eyes widened and the hair on the back of his neck began to rise. In a manner of seconds all his hair was standing on end and he seemed twice as big as he was. He looked fearsome. Had I been a tom cat I would have been looking for cover.

After he had puffed himself up to full battle size, he began coming up the steps. A mighty growl began to come from way down deep inside him somewhere, and as he cleared the last step he bowed his neck and began angling across the porch.

But that Siamese was full of surprises. He didn't head for cover. His back arched, and his blue-crossed eyes seemed to be looking in two directions at once as he stepped out to meet Pasquali.

Then he let out the weirdest, the most frightening, god-awfullest yowl that Pasquali and I had ever heard. It froze him in his tracks, just as it did me. And as that skinny little Siamese with those crazy eyes that didn't seem to focus on anything advanced, the insults he screamed at Pasquali grew louder and louder.

For about 30 seconds Pasquali held his ground. Then he began to deflate. As his hair flattened out I knew the courage he had mustered coming up the steps had deserted him. After the Siamese had taken two more steps, Pasquali turned and bolted from the porch. There was no slinking around about it, either. He just flat took off.

It was the finest display of propagandizing I've ever seen. I'm sure Pasquali could have wiped that scrawny little Siamese out in 30 seconds if he hadn't howled and yowled him full of fright. It's too bad the Siamese wasn't working for the U.S. government diplomatic corps. He could have accomplished twice as much as a dozen statesmen in half the time.

But I didn't hold it against Pasquali. If that Siamese had glanced once in my direction, I would have been right behind him. I might even have been in front of him. When that Siamese began to squall you just naturally wanted to be out in front.

# Animal Relationships

I haven't heard of a lion bedding down with a lamb, unless the lamb was inside the lion. But animals do strike up strange relationships. I've observed a number of them.

I've seen dogs and cats become good friends, to all appearances at least. And I've seen cats that apparently had no objection to tame white mice tripping through their territory. But I must admit, I was never quite sure about feline sincerity in such cases.

That sleepy, dreamy look cats get in their eyes always made me wonder about the eventual fate of the mice. Fat cats usually know who's going to get it next. They usually know where the next meal is coming from.

Once I saw a black bear cub and an old wooly collie dog develop a friendship — of sorts. But the cub enjoyed it much more than the tired old dog. He constantly tormented the collie. When he was trying to nap, the cub would sneak up and yank his tail. And when the dog came up snapping and snarling the bear would scuttle off, his eyes gleaming with mischievous joy.

But the old dog had his day. When the cub got a little bigger he got too rough and rambunctious. Since all the zoos had more black bears than they needed, the fellow who had raised the roly-poly little bruin took him back in the woods and set him free.

He had no idea he was supposed to be a wild bear, and when some loggers showed up for work one morning he went to greet them. They had no idea he was a tame bear, so they shot him and the old collie snoozed peacefully ever after.

Once we had a momma rabbit that adopted some kittens. They lost their mother the morning she darted out in front of a car as she was crossing the road. The rabbit took care of them until they got big enough to drink milk from a dish.

She was somewhat puzzled by the kittens. I'm sure she knew they were different, but she didn't kick them out. With tender maternal compassion she did her duty. She was the epitome of kindness, tolerance and generosity.

Strange as that was, this is even stranger. Our neighbor, Linda Weaver, is still a little confused, but repetition finally convinced her that she actually saw what she had seen.

However, she wasn't sure the morning she went into the barn and saw what she thought was a dead mouse lying beside a nest her chickens had hollowed out in the straw. But it wasn't a mouse at all. It was a kitten.

And in the nest was Misty, her neighbor's calico cat who had traveled a quarter of a mile to have four kittens there. As far as Linda was concerned that was okay. She had three kids of her own. She knows how it is.

But when she checked the next morning to see how Misty and her family was doing, she was in for a surprise. In the nest with them were two eggs. Now Linda knows that cats have kittens, and she is almost certain they don't lay eggs. But for a moment she was shaken. She thought Mother Nature had thrown her a curve.

As it turned out, two of her hens had exercised their proprietary rights and continued to use the nest even though it had been turned into a feline maternity ward. And the old mother cat didn't seem to mind when they hopped in and laid their eggs on top of her and the kittens.

I wonder what the reaction of the hens will be when momma and her brood move out. They may go on strike. Once you've enjoyed a fur-lined nest you certainly don't want to settle for less.

# Somebody is a Little Mixed-up

We have a cat with a long ringed tail, short soft hair and big yellow tiger-like eyes. She came to us quite unexpectedly.

One morning about three years ago I looked out as the dog tore across the yard the way he did when a strange cat invaded his domain, and there she was.

But she didn't whirl and run the way most cats did when Grover charged them like a Sherman tank. She didn't even get excited. She greeted him with a friendly sweep of her tail. And while he stood there with his tongue hanging out in pink dismay, she arched her back daintily, sat down and began washing her face.

Grover was completely baffled. Finally he sat down to watch her complete her morning toilet.

When she was through, she gave him a bright-eyed look and flicked him coyly with her tail as she started for the house. It was plain to see that she was a female. With wiles like that, she had to be.

We don't know where she came from. She probably got separated from her owners when they stopped their car along the highway. Obviously she was someone's pet. She convinced us with her friendly self-assurance that she had been well treated.

I named her Momma Kitty. During the first spring she was here, it seemed noisily appropriate. There was much yowling of tomcats in the dark of night, and fits and fights of various kinds. Obviously, she was going to be a proud parent before too long. But to our surprise, Momma Kitty didn't deliver.

Nor has she. Either Nature went on strike, or I made a mistake. I have a sneaking hunch I'm the one who goofed. A couple of times

Momma Kitty has stretched with the languid indifference that old tomcats practice.

I hope I'm wrong about not being right. If Momma Kitty turns out to be a neutered male, I'll never live it down. If she turns out to be a Poppa Kitty I wonder if he'll adopt a set of borrowed kittens long enough to prove me right.

Maybe such things run in our family. My sister Nancy had a similar experience. When her oldest son, Rocky, went off to college, he left his parakeet for her to take care of. His name was Rooster.

For a long time Rooster lived peacefully in his cage. He spent his days flitting from perch to perch and back again. He didn't seem to mind. He was like people you see every day, aimless and unconcerned as long as someone else is supplying their needs.

But one day Nancy noticed that he was tearing up the paper in the bottom of his cage. While raising a husband and two boys, she decided that males often do things that defy explanation, and she wasn't at all surprised by Rooster's odd behavior. But after a couple months of such nonsense, she was getting a little aggravated.

Her husband, Chuck, told her Rooster was just trying to turn the paper over so he could read the other side. When he told Rooster it wouldn't do any good because one side was as bad as the other, Rooster went into a shredding frenzy. If he'd had it, Nancy said, he could have gone through a Sunday edition of the New York Times in nothing flat.

Then Rooster did the impossible — the unthinkable. In a nest of shredded paper he'd built, he laid three eggs, and Nancy was ecstatic. "What a rare bird," she exclaimed. "A male parakeet that lays eggs." She'd never heard of such a thing. She thought Rooster should be in the Guinness Book of Records.

Mother received the news that Rooster was sitting proudly on three tiny eggs with soft laughter. "That's good," she told Nancy. "It gives him something to do."

My mother soon will be 82, and she knows a lot about time and the way it stacks up when it gets stale. If Nancy knew as much about birds, Rooster would never have laid eggs.

And if I'd known as much about cats, Momma Kitty would have been a mother more times than I care to think about. And she wouldn't be sitting around looking as smug as he does — and that's for sure.

# Bird-Brained?

In front of our car, a big four-wheel-drive pickup was parked. In the grillwork, just above the shiny bumper, were two slots about eight inches long and two inches high.

While I was sitting there, a sparrow landed on the bumper. After jerkily looking around, it bobbed through one of the slots and disappeared.

I straightened up. I knew it was going to be trouble, and I tried to see behind the grille. I couldn't. If the driver showed up while I was there, I was going to tell him about the sparrow. If he lifted the hood, I figured, it could escape.

I didn't need to concern myself. Just after I had reached that conclusion, the sparrow reappeared in the opposite slot, with a small butterfly in its beak. It had picked it off the radiator, where bugs collect when a vehicle is moving. That's the way it looked, but I still didn't believe it. Sparrows are not that smart.

But they are. Another one soon slipped by on its way to inspect a late model automobile. It hopped around on the bumper, but it had no luck. The openings in the grille were too small for it to get through. With an impudent flip of its tail, it took off, presumably to find a grille more generously endowed.

In a few minutes a sparrow again landed on the bumper of the pickup and dipped through one of the slots. Moments later it reappeared on the other side with a moth in its beak. After a quick glance around, it buzzed away.

I watched in amazement. Those sparrows were smart enough to be in a government think tank. Maybe they were too smart to be in one, I don't know. But they weren't alone.

Not long after that I was mowing hay in a field pimpled with ant hills. If left alone they grow and grow, and when the sickle mows into one it's a startling experience. So it won't break, a quick release on the mower allows the sickle bar to swing back when it meets an immoveable object. And it does. When it bites into one of those ant hills, it yaws around like a broken arm.

I usually go out in the spring and level them. But I missed one and when the mower hit it the war was on. Out of that sickled hill came thousands of angry ants.

I was thankful I could reset the release without getting off the tractor. They would have devoured me in an instant. They would have digested me with glee.

In the field at the time was a flock of blackbirds. They usually congregate when a mower moves into a field because they know a good thing when they see it. They feast on the bugs that burst like bullets out of the hay as it begins to fall.

After I had driven off one of them discovered the hill, which was boiling over with ants, and began loading up. As I came by on another round it took off, made a big loop in the sky, zig zagged across the field and came swooping back.

Each time another bird approached it did the same thing. Apparently it was trying to conceal its discovery by acting like it hadn't discovered anything at all. So don't sell blackbirds short. They're smart. And here's a woodpecker that was no dummy.

A friend of ours watched it go up one side of a small tree in his yard with its beak hammering like a staple gun. When it reached a certain limb, it reversed direction and came hammering back down the other side of the tree. After completing the cycle it waited a few minutes, then went at it again.

When he checked, Bill found a string of ants going up the tree. They had found something they liked on one of the leaves and were trying to get it back to the hill. But they weren't having much luck. The woodpecker was dry gulching them along the trail.

If that's what being bird-brained is all about, I'll take some. I'll take a whole bunch if there's enough to go around. I could use it.

# Memories of an Elk

On a warm sunny afternoon a couple of weeks ago I was feeding the cows in a small field next to the barn. As I was going after another bale of hay, I saw an elk coming down through the pasture. It was a cow, and she was coming slowly, timidly, because she was on strange terrain.

Elk don't have the fine-boned grace that deer have, but they have a distinct nobility of carriage — a sort of regalness. And they are a perfect blend of browns and grays, which quickly dissolves into an autumn scene. She was a beautiful animal.

Even after she had seen me, she came on through the pasture. She was watchful, but not fearful. After she had jumped the fence into the small field where the cows were eating, she strolled along the fence that separates our place from the neighbors. When she jumped that fence she began strolling toward the highway.

Apparently the traffic scared her, and she turned back. As she began running, her legs seemed to rotate like wheels — or so it seemed — and she glided over the ground. When she slowed, she began walking toward the neighbor's cows. But they didn't have any desire to consort with an elk. They threw up their heads and took off on a dead run.

With the field glasses I saw that her mouth was open, and her sides were heaving. She had been chased hard by something — dogs perhaps — and she must have been confused. I guess she mistook our cows for the herd she was looking for. I watched until she dissolved into the trees near the back of our place.

Now it is another time — a time long past. It is late fall on a wet, grey, rainy wind-whipped day and I have the dogs. There are two.

Spud is big and black and busy, and Sam is lean and rangy, a hound with long ears and a deep mellow voice that can be heard for miles when he hits a trail.

I am high on a timbered hillside to start a deer that will run by my dad and a neighbor who are waiting with rifles in different places along the trail deer follow to the river.

As I angle across the face of the hill, Sam's long spiky tail begins whipping around in circles as he zig-zags back and forth in front of me. Then Spud lets out an excited yip and veers sharply up the hill. With a mighty bellow Sam takes off after him.

I listen to Sam's voice as it rises higher and higher on the hill. The deer is trying to elude them, but I know it will turn eventually and head for the river. If I hurry I might be there when it arrives.

It is steep ground and I've slipped and slithered halfway down the hill when I hear Sam's mournful voice riding lightly on the wind. The deer has turned, and I move faster. I want to be there. I might even get a shot at it.

When I hear the rifle I know it's too late. I expect to see a deer stretched out in the small clearing where dad has been waiting, but he is gone and I charge down the hill. I catch up with him and our neighbor Bill, who figures he hit the deer with the only shot he got. Ahead we hear the dogs.

The deer is in the river. It is standing belly deep in water. It is trying to fight off the snarling, snapping dogs. It's been hit and it's woozy. When it wobbles and goes down, the dogs charge and we splash out to get it before they do. It isn't a pretty sight. A clean kill is one thing, but this is cruel and brutal.

That's the memory the elk brought back as she slowly crossed the field. A few years after that I quit hunting and I wanted to forget all about it. But she wouldn't let me.

As I took another look I decided that forgetting is such an easy out. It absolves us of our injustices. It cleanses us of dirt we've never shed. If short memories are an absolution, failure to remember may be the gravest crime of all.

# Wrestling Bear Became a Farce

The bear was a sad sight. He was old and scruffy, listless and bleary eyed. His owner tried to create the illusion that he was a ferocious, man-eating beast, but he didn't have much luck. The old bruin was too tired to go along with the deceit.

I saw him in a little town on a hot summer afternoon. He was an attraction in a carnival. "The Mighty Wrestling Bear" would take on all comers, said his owner, as the bear sagged down on his haunches and gazed with tired indifference out over the crowd that had gathered around the ring that stood in front of a faded tent.

The bear's teeth had been pulled, and his claws had been yanked out. He had been deliberately neutralized. A kitten would have been more dangerous.

I waited around to watch him perform against one of the local muscle men who was to get $25 if he stayed with him for a specified number of minutes. The challenger had been well fortified with booze by the time he crawled into the ring.

The bear probably weighed 250 pounds, and when his trainer yanked on the chain fastened to his leg he waddled out to meet his courageous opponent. He reared up as they neared the center of the ring and collapsed on the boozy grappler.

For a minute or so he squirmed helplessly around on the mat while the bear held him down. When the trainer yanked the chain the bear let him up and immediately pinned him again. He did it slowly and mechanically. He was the only dignified part of the performance.

83

Later, I saw another wrestling bear perform. He was younger, and his hair was smooth and thick and shiny. His eyes were bright and he moved with graceful stealth. I remembered the old bear as I watched him prowl restlessly at the end of his chain. "Gus the Wrestling Bear" looked like a worthy opponent.

He wasn't there to wrestle a psyched-up novice out of the crowd. Gus had made the big time. He was the main attraction at the weekly wrestling matches held in the local armory.

With Gorgeous George and The Great Atlas and The Toledo Terror he shared top billing. No slouch was Gus. And he had all his teeth, and his claws. He looked formidable enough to leave alone.

But that changed shortly. After he had been muzzled with a contraption that resembled a catcher's mask, he didn't look so awesome. And after his claws had been rendered harmless by leather socks strapped over his feet, he began to look about half benign.

Matched against him were a couple of wrestlers whose bag of tricks included all the illegal holds they could imagine. It was to be an exciting bout. The meanies matched against the deadly beast, all muzzled and manacled.

To win, the wrestlers had to stay in the ring 10 minutes with Gus. The crowd hooted and howled as they strutted around the ring and flexed their muscles while waiting for the bell to ring.

They didn't fare very well against Gus, and the fans roared with joy. They love underdogs even when they're bears. And they soared into seventh heaven when Gus got confused and turned on the referee.

Nothing seems to warm the human heart quicker than authority on the run, especially when it is being pursued by a shaggy black bruin that doesn't know the difference between a referee and a refried bean.

As the defeated wrestlers made their sullen way through the taunting crowd, Gus was stripped of his muzzle and gloves. As the crowd cheered, he lifted a bottle of pop and swizzled it down. Then he was led from the ring. He was panting. He was hot and bothered.

It was all a farce. Gus had been reduced to a parody of himself, just as the old bear had been. When animals are stripped of their dignity to provide burlesque spectacles they become pathetic. But never as pathetic as those who make them that way.

# The Dark Side of the Mind

Students at the University of Nebraska built a big bonfire, according to an Associated Press story that appeared in a Sunday edition of the Statesman-Journal in 1981. They fueled it with trash, furniture, and anything else they could find. To add a little fat to the fire they threw in some live chickens.

Why live chickens?

Who knows. And at a university at that, where you would expect to find a more sensitive, less degraded atmosphere prevailing. Chickens are not very highly regarded on anyone's scale of sympathies. I'm well aware of that. But when they are treated so cruelly they become a symbol of something else.

They symbolize that deep, dark corner of the human mind which finds a morbid satisfaction in that which repels. Although it is repugnant, cruelty does attract. Ever since he established dominion over the creatures of the earth, birds and animals have been victims of man's perversion. And that's what cruelty is: A perversion, a sickness for which there doesn't appear to be a cure.

How can anyone derive pleasure from cutting the feet off a trapped squirrel? I don't know, but I know a fellow who did. Then he turned it loose. I can still hear that squirrel squealing as he said it did. I can see it tumbling off in a frantic attempt to run. All too vividly I can see it falling back from the tree it tried time and again to climb because it had no front feet to climb it with.

I asked him why he did it, and he said he didn't know. He wasn't remorseful. He wasn't sorry. And he wasn't a bad guy. In every respect but that one he seemed to be an average normal person. That's the way it is with evil, it seems. It has such a clever facility for disguise.

It's a strange thing, cruelty. No one knows from what twisted corner of the soul it springs. But there is something fiendishly frightening about a compulsion to torture something just to watch it recoil in anguished terror. There is something kinked completely out of shape in a person's head who does such things. But how did it become so kinked?

Can it begin by inflicting pain as punishment? I've often wondered. There seems to be something insidious about the process. The old adage that you can get used to anything seems to apply.

I've heard people who had never been around livestock say they would never hurt a thing. I've watched those same people lay the whip on plenty heavy in the name of punishment after they had been around them for a while. And they got used to doing it. They weren't torturing animals, that's obvious. But gradually their sensibilities had become blunted.

I believe that violence on TV has the same effect. And it is more pernicious because it doesn't involve the viewer directly. He doesn't have to get his hands bloody. He is spared the grisly sights and sounds. They are censored, and that which should be repulsive becomes more commonplace.

Prolonged exposure to violence, it seems to me, dulls the conscience, and after a while it shrugs indifferently at the degradation of man or beast. Is it any wonder that propaganda has become such a force in the world?

Cruelty cheapens life. Whether it's violence on TV, a squirrel being maimed, or chickens being burned alive in some senseless, springtime ritual, it makes no difference. But the attitude that permits its practice, and the attitude that condones it makes a difference. It may make the BIG difference in time to come. When life, any form of life, is treated with such senseless disregard we had better take another look at things because even you and I can be disregarded.

# BUYING AND SELLING

# A Roundup That Went Wild

The cattle were wild. We knew that. We also knew that several before us had tried to round them up without success. But we decided we might just be able to do what the others hadn't. If we had only known.

They were Whiteface cattle, strong from running up and down the hills, and they knew all the tricks. They had gone wild several years before, after the owner had turned them out to pasture in the foothills that roll down out of the Cascades to meet the Willamette Valley. Some of the cows, which had been calves then, now had calves. Since they were too wild to count, no one knew how many there were.

Those who had tried to corral them before had built a big pole pen in a meadow at the foot of the hills. Angling off from the gate was a drift fence about a quarter of a mile long. We figured if we could get the cattle crowded up against the fence we could shoot them into the corral at a dead run.

It took several hours to get them down out of the hills. They were wise, those cattle were, and they would stand like statues in the brush until you had ridden on by them. We could only get one or two at a time, which we bunched in the meadow because it is easier to drive a herd than one or two wild, ornery critters. It took two men on horses to keep them there while the others were brought in.

By late afternoon, we had collected between 40 and 50 head. The run through the hills didn't seem to bother them much, and they watched us with what I can only describe as calculated arrogance. Since they had played this game before, they seemed to feel they had the edge on us. And the calves frisked around as though they actually enjoyed it.

We didn't. We were tired. Our horses were lathered with sweat. They were breathing hard, and we decided to give them a rest before we started the big push. They were going to be stove up for a week after it was over, and so were their riders.

When the time came to get on with it, we crawled back in the saddles. Slowly we surrounded the cattle and began easing them toward the drift fence. All went well for a ways. Too well. They seemed to be going along with the gag, which surprised me. Except for a calf or two, eager to show us what they could do, the cattle turned and headed for the corral when they hit the fence.

It was the lull before the storm.

Soon they began picking up speed. Then they were running along the fence. Hooves began thundering as they broke into a dead run. The wind roared in our ears and we headed for the corral, hell bent for election.

Four of us were riding on the outside, hazing them into the fence, and another rider was bringing up the rear. For a moment it looked as though we were going to succeed.

But suddenly, a cow veered off and broke away. Another followed her. More did the same, and there was no stopping them. They had horns and knew how to use them. The horses knew that too, and refused to hold their ground. I don't blame them. Being ventilated by a set of horns is not the happiest of prospects.

All the whooping and hollering and the mighty fine cursing did no good that day. When it was all over, we had corralled two old cows that had been too slow to keep up with the rest. They weren't much of a prize.

As we stood around the corral listening to the horses catch their breath, I asked Billie, a wizened little old cowboy, how far east those cattle could go.

He squinted up at the mountains drowsing in the late afternoon sun as he wiped the sweat off his face. "Those dirty, onery blankety-blank ying-yangs can go plumb to sagebrush," he said disgustedly.

They probably did. I wouldn't be surprised if they are still running wild somewhere in Central Oregon today.

# Horse Trading

Horse trading is a fine art. There's nothing simple about it. A good horse trader must be an expert at whittling, straw chewing, neck scratching, thoughtful, well-aimed spitting and serious staring and studying. And he must know how to make time go a long way. A deal that doesn't last at least half a day can hardly be called a deal at all.

It also requires a variety of subtle insinuations, which can be taken for back-handed compliments by the uninitiated and those susceptible to flattery. Horse traders are super psychologists. The ones I knew could out-shrink a shrink, 10 to 1. Most of the time they could do the same thing to the guy they were dealing with, 100 to 1.

Old Red was a master of the subtle insinuation. He relied upon it to a great degree, but he didn't look like the psychological type. He was a grizzled little trader with red hair, sharp blue eyes all squinched up at the corners, and white eyebrows.

One day in the heat of a big trade I heard him say to one of his potential victims: "Mister, I been to two county fairs and clean across the state of Texas, but I never seen anybody could deal like y'all can. Dadburned if I don't believe you'd take advantage of old Red if he'd give you half a chance."

Needless to say, he didn't have a chance. Old Red hadn't been to two county fairs and clean across the state of Texas for nothing. And nothing was about all the guy had left when old Red got through with him.

Sometimes the insinuations were not so cleverly veiled. J.B. demonstrated that as he was trying to put a deal together one day. He was a tall, lanky trader with a long leathery face that was forever screwed up in a puzzled frown as though he was never quite sure what was going on. I thought for a long time he had trouble with his eyes, until I found out it was just an act to hide a fine, conniving mind.

But he wasn't doing too well on this particular day. The fellow he was dickering with was no slouch. I hadn't seen him before but he had a heart well equipped with larceny. When J.B. saw that things were not going his way, he crawled up and settled down on the top board of the corral fence.

"I never did have high hopes of getting to heaven," he said as he stared down at the horses involved in the trade, "but once I tell St. Peter I been trying to deal with you he'll probably give me the best room in the place."

"Get a permanent lease on it if you can," said the little skinny guy he was trying to skin, "or you ain't gonna last long. Once he finds out about you trying to pass this spavined old nag off as sound he'll send you down where Coca-Cola don't stay cool."

I doubt that St. Peter admitted either one of them. If he did he should have been fired, summarily. A pair like that would have had all the gold in heaven cornered in a week.

It didn't happen often, but once in a while one of them would take a loss. Oscar did, but it wasn't really his fault. He was a victim of circumstances beyond his control.

With his machine-gun gift of gab he could make any old nag sound like Man of War reincarnated. And that's what he intended to do with the sick horse he left in our corral one night because he didn't want to haul it any further until he had a chance to doctor it up. It was plain to see that some unsuspecting soul was about to get an education.

The next morning we were checking some cattle. When we noticed a couple that needed shots, we discovered we didn't have any penicillin. As Oscar breezed into the barn we asked him if he had any.

"Hell yeah," he said. "I got two bottles. I was going to give 'em to that pinto out there, but the so-and-so laid down and died before I got a chance to."

There were two good things about that: The horse was out of its misery, and someone had been spared a costly lesson. And Oscar had bought a dead horse, which was something I had never expected to see. To the seven wonders of the world, an eighth had been added.

# Recollections of
# One Home's Showpiece

Look over there, in front of that second-hand store. At that chrome dinette set. The one with four chairs and the design on top that looks like an hour glass.

I know that set. I know it well. I probably sold it. At what auction, I wonder. In what state? In what town?

Was it Prosser? Or Sandpoint? Hermiston? Ogden, perhaps? Or Yuba City?

I don't remember. But it's good merchandise. Douglas chrome ware. And that's a formica-type top, folks, that won't scar, burn, blemish or blister. And it hasn't. It was a buy. A bargain.

So what is it doing here, waiting forlornly out in front of the store today, the table and four chairs that stand like spindly-legged waifs looking for a pat on their faded backs.

By what route did they get here? When did they slip from new to old? At what moment? At what meal? What day was one too many?

That's the small set. For $30 folks could have the large one. The one with six chairs. The chrome-plated model with the big red design on top instead of the small black one.

But that was as big as they needed. And they were happy, the folks that bought that set out there. They were proud. And they knew they'd got a bargain. They were pleased as punch.

And the kids wrestled to rip the boxes apart so they could see if the one inside looked like the "real one" they had bought at auction. And momma smiled like one who'd waited a long time for a dream to come true. Even dad grinned a little sheepishly at what his generosity had done.

91

Yes sir, a real bargain at $37.50.

Then it was loaded and it was gone. Out of sight and out of mind. And on down the road we go with more happiness for sale.

Somewhere back there that chrome dinette set became the showpiece of some kitchen, which is the finest room in any house. They draw people, kitchens do. Their warmth does it. They generate fellowship and good smells. They bake in deep ovens and bubble in big pots. They brown and bake and baste. Of all the rooms they are best.

Where better to be center stage. It's no wonder they take their places so proudly: new table and four new chairs. They know they are important.

"Keep your feet off," momma says. "Don't set that hot pan on the table. Don't spill . . . Don't scratch . . . Don't, don't, don't."

Is it any wonder they stand so smug in all their glory?

Meals taste better too. And momma smiles more. And homework isn't half so hard when it's worked on that slick, shiny top. And those padded seats sure are nice and soft. Not hard as a rock like those old wooden chairs.

But momma shakes her head. "No," she says, "can't have them for a playhouse. Got to save those old chairs for company because we've never got enough to go around."

New table and chairs gather for all important conferences. They patiently serve during the long hours it takes to decide what to do about the car, "since it's startin' to run a little rough." Or the truck. Or the roof that's beginning to leak. Or the pump.

With steadfast devotion to duty they endure as a stubby pencil scratches away at a scribbled page where figures line up in scraggly rows. And they hear the hopeless sigh because there's never enough at the bottom line to go around. But they're there, the table and four chairs, to support those weighty, hard-to-make decisions.

They've held up through trials and tribulations, despair and despondency. They've heard laughter too, knew joy, and shared happiness.

If so loyal, how come . . . ?

Sold when? To whom?

But why try to revive the past. The days of glory are gone. Second-hand time is time to put the memories away.

# Dignity Frequents
# the Oddest Places

There were four of them in a row: shacky little cabins standing so close to a big marsh that water nearly surrounded them in the winter when it rained.

Jess, a tall, slow moving fellow with a long sad face and drooping shoulders, owned them. He owned property everywhere. He didn't look very shrewd, but he was. Someone said he became stooped carrying all that money to the bank every week.

If that was so, those tacky little cabins increased his burden. When high-classed apartments in town were begging for occupants, they were full. The turn-over among his tenants was rather high, but there were plenty waiting to move in when someone moved out.

To minimize losses, Jess insisted that rent be paid in advance. But he was flexible. He would take anything in lieu of money, if there was enough of it. I met him when he began selling some of his collateral through an auction we were running.

Tires, tools, guns, fishing equipment, musical instruments — he wasn't particular as long as it paid the rent, plus a little more. Since he had to peddle the stuff before he got his money, he figured he was entitled to a bonus. Rarely did he fail to collect one.

He told me those four old shacks made him more money than anything he owned. He spent just enough on maintenance to keep them liveable, which meant they were in such sad shape taxes were practically nil. He couldn't lose.

Some people criticized his mode of operation. They claimed he was taking advantage of the poor, the dispossessed and down-and-outers, but he shrugged them off.

"If I didn't have places like those they wouldn't have a place to stay," he said, "unless you want to put them up."

I had never been in them until one of Jess' tenants called me. In a soft drawl he asked if I would consider buying some stuff he had to sell. When I asked him why he didn't call Jess, he hummed and hawed around so long I decided he had already dealt with Jess in a way that hadn't been too gratifying.

When I pulled up in front of the shack, he and his wife stepped out to meet me. They were probably in their early 20's. They had come west from the hills of the deep South to improve their lot in life, he said, but they hadn't had much luck. To get by till things got better they needed to sell some of their belongings.

As he talked their six kids swarmed like busy little bees around a toothless, wrinkled old woman wearing a loose, blue flowery dress. She was their grandmother, I was told, mother of their mother.

From a doorway that opened into one of the other two rooms, the old lady listened as he named the items they felt they could get by without. She looked tired and weary and worn out. Her daughter and son-in-law were taking things in stride, but she was ashamed of the plight they were in.

"Mr. Smith," she said in a quiet, tentative voice, "can I talk with y'all a minute?"

Such formality sounded ludicrous in that dilapidated shack. I could hardly keep from laughing as her son-in-law stepped through the door she was waiting to close. It was hardly the place for high faluting airs.

When he came out he was holding a brooch. That was her contribution. It was an heirloom, he said, that had been passed down through her family. It was a measure of their desperation.

I bought the other stuff, but not the brooch. I told him I didn't have any idea what it was worth, which I didn't. I hope she never had to sell it, but I have a feeling it wound up in a pawn shop somewhere.

That was a touching incident. I realize now that the old lady was trying to dignify with formality circumstances that hurt her pride. It no longer seems ludicrous or laughable.

# Meals for the Memory

I'm no gourmet. I haven't got a cultivated taste. I wouldn't recognize a crepe suzette if I saw one coming down Interstate 5, unless it was wearing vanity license plates that said so. I never saw a pheasant under glass, except in museums where pheasants under glass belong. And what's a lobster thermidor? And why do they need one anyway?

Despite a palate that can barely tell sweet from sour, there have been meals I remember. They stick in my mind like peanut butter. One I had in Clarkston, Washington, just across the Snake River from Lewiston, Idaho, is one I keep going back to enjoy. What a treat it was.

But I prepared for it. I'd had no breakfast that morning because I had to get an early start and didn't get started early enough to eat. It was a cold miserable day in early spring, and two of us were going to Grangeville, Idaho to hold an auction.

All day long we were about an hour behind the clock, and when it came time for lunch we didn't have time for it. So we managed the best we could on coffee that an old thermos did its best to keep lukewarm.

By the time we were through it was late in the afternoon, and everything had closed except the bars. So we headed back to Lewiston, which was about 50 miles north of there, via a road full of tortured curves.

Since we were going to work in Washington the next day, we drove on into Clarkston and got a motel. After we had cleaned up, we went looking for a place to eat. The place we found was the first one we came to. It was dark and dingy, a hole-in-the-wall restaurant in front and a bar in back. If we hadn't been so hungry we probably wouldn't have stopped. I'm glad we did.

The steak I had there was the best I've ever eaten. It was thick and juicy. On the outside it had been seared a dark brown. On the inside it had been broiled a pale pink. It was covered with mushrooms swimming in a tangy sauce. I sat there and savored the aroma as long as I could, then I grabbed a knife and fork.

The first bite was better than the smell. And the second was better than the first. When I close my eyes and lean back I can still see, smell it, taste it till it's gone. And then I'm sorry.

Why can't such things go on forever? Why can't life be one fine steak buried in mushrooms as long as we live?

The gustatory experience I had in a bright and cheery Susanville, California restaurant wasn't quite as tastefully scintillating. I'm not even sure that's the way to describe the waffles I wrestled there one morning as a big glassy sun rolled up on the horizon.

They were a little pale around the gills when they arrived, but I didn't pay much attention. I thought maybe it was an illusion caused by the sun reflecting off the window. But I knew the sun didn't make them taste the way they did. That could only result from some grave omission by the cook. Or perhaps it was due to some grave addition, because they resembled corrugated spastic plastic.

They didn't submit. They were tough and resilient. Once you got a bite in your mouth it bounced around like a ping-pong ball. You didn't chew them. You were lucky if you could even capture one.

Finally I gave up. I told the waitress I didn't have the stamina to eat breakfast there. She nodded curtly and swished away. She didn't even try to conceal her contempt for customers who gave up so easily. I apologized in the best way I knew how. I left her a sizeable tip to make amends and slipped out as unnoticed as I could go.

There is one thing about hunger: it works. Absence may not make the heart grow fonder in love, but if you're hungry it will make you greedy as a hog. By the time I had traveled down the road a ways, I was sorry I hadn't given that waffle my best shot. I tried to appease my growling stomach with thoughts of that steak I'd had in Clarkston, but it demanded more than memories.

# WHO COULD
# FORGET THEM?

# A Lesson in
# the Color of Hatred

When I stepped out on the highway at Shafter, California, and raised my thumb it was six o'clock in the morning and 103 degrees. I was heading north, I'd had all the hot weather I wanted. It was June, and I was looking forward to some Oregon cool.

The road stretched straight as a string through the valley and cars shot by with a sound like ripping canvas. Hundreds of them must have passed during the hour I stood there, and the sun was beginning to do its stuff. I was beginning to sweat it out when a big, long Oldsmobile came to a screeching halt after it had passed me at full speed. I had to run a quarter-mile to reach it, but I was grateful.

The fellow driving was black, and I was surprised. It was 1949 and I hadn't expected to see a black guy driving a car that fancy. I hadn't expected one to pick me up, either. I hesitated before I crawled in.

It turned out that he was as uneasy with me as I was with him. We didn't say much, but after a few miles he reached under the seat and pulled out a pint of whiskey. He offered me a drink, but I declined. It was pretty early in the day to be hitting the hard stuff.

He was from Los Angeles, he said, and he was going to San Francisco to try out for the San Francisco Seals, which was a professional baseball team.

Pretty soon he asked me if I could drive. When he asked me if I would, I decided the car was stolen. But I figured I could talk my way out of that quicker than I could out of a wreck if he kept drinking and driving. So we changed places, and he curled up in the corner of the front seat and went to sleep.

When he woke up he rubbed his eyes. They were blood-shot and tired looking. When I suggested that we get something to eat, he nodded. As we drifted through the outskirts of a little town I pulled up in front of a small white cafe. He followed me across the parking lot.

As we entered I noticed the quiet. But I didn't think much about it, even though everyone was watching us. I didn't realize what was going on until I saw the cold hard look in the waitress' eyes as she slapped the menus down in front of us.

That was before any serious attempt had been made to end discrimination, and I had violated the unwritten rule by bringing my benefactor into the cafe. For him she had contempt. For me she reserved a special brand of hatred. I was the traitor. It was a strange experience. A little frightening. I'm still surprised she didn't refuse to serve us. I wonder why she didn't.

By the time we got to San Francisco it was dark, and I decided to catch a bus. I had a little money, and I didn't want to spend the rest of the night standing beside some deserted road. But he didn't know his way around Frisco any better than I did, which meant that we were lost.

He drove for more than an hour, up and down those steep, tilted streets, until we found the bus depot. By then we were friends. I would have fought for him, and I'm sure he would've done the same for me. He wasn't black anymore, and I wasn't white. We were just a couple of guys that had come together for a few hours because Fate decided we should meet.

I dropped $5 in the seat as I got out. He started to protest, but I shook my head. He extended his hand and squeezed mine hard. I never saw him again.

I still don't know whether that car was his. And I don't know if he was in San Francisco to try out for the Seals. But thanks to him I know how it feels to be hated by someone who had no reason to hate me. And because of him, I know how absurd such hatred is.

# Lifetime Goes on the Auction Block

Recently we disposed of a lifetime. I think that's the best way to describe it. We got rid of it at auction.

It was a long life, too. The old man whose estate we sold had lived for nearly 90 years. He had lived on the same place for more than 50. Before her death a few years before, his wife had shared it with him.

He had been a machinist and an inventor. He had worked for years as a millwright. He had been interested in fly fishing, movie making, taxidermy and a number of other things that alert, active minds take pleasure in.

I didn't know him well. I met him only once, and I was never on his place until after he had died.

But he didn't need to be there to tell you about those things. The clues were everywhere. They had been carefully put away in drawers. They had been wrapped in newspapers and laid on shelves. They had been catalogued in paper cartons. They had been boxed and put away.

His shop was filled with the specialized tools of his trade. One that was used to take teeth out of big circular saws hung on the wall. Not many people knew what it was. On a shelf above the work bench in the rear was a grinder for sharpening those curved steel teeth. Most people looked and speculated. "Looks like a can opener to me," said one bemused woman.

There were tool chests he had made, with dovetailed corners and trays that could be lifted out to reveal more trays below. In one corner was an antique pie safe with pierced tin doors that he had filled with assorted nuts and bolts long before it had become an antique.

In the adjoining room were stands he had made to hold long wooden rollers he had designed as a curtain stretcher for his wife. It was craftmanship that precision, long smooth lines and graceful curves had elevated to an art form. It was easy to see that a man who believed in doing things right had lived there.

In the shed beside the house was wood he had cut and stacked. Some had been there a long time. Lying on a worn old chopping block was the hatchet he had used to split kindling. The wood sold for $120, the hatchet for $5. Before the sale was over, most of the wood had been hauled away.

In a small chest he had stored a valuable collection of Indian artifacts. Bracelets, beads, baskets, bowls, moccasins and a baby's beaded leggins had been carefully packed away. Not so carefully, they were unpacked. As they were sold, they scattered quickly among the crowd.

I hope he wasn't watching. I would hate to think he witnessed the callous way that people bargained for things he'd treasured. I wouldn't want him to think that all his life had been reduced to that.

And I'm glad he wasn't there to see his movie projector sold. It didn't bring much. It was an old-timer that technology had rendered obsolete. With it was a large screen. With the screen was a film splicer he had made from spools on which thread had been wound. Wherever I looked, I saw him.

Then came the guns: rifles and shotguns. I don't hunt, but I appreciate guns. And he had some outstanding ones, expensive models that were displayed in a gun cabinet with leaded glass doors he had made. They had sleek, smooth lines. They had dark blue barrels and glossy stocks and forearms. They represented a connoisseur's selection. In minutes they were gone.

In the corner was the hospital bed he had been confined to for months before he died. It was bought by a fellow who had bad hips. He said he had just as well get prepared because he knew he was going to need it sooner or later.

The sale was nearly over, and I glanced into the pantry. Hanging on a nail behind the door was a red plaid jacket and an old, greasy, crumpled-up felt hat. I didn't touch them. They were still hanging there when I left.

Within hours it was all over. Things that had been permanent for so long became transient in a matter of minutes. In bits and pieces his life was hauled away. By the next day his identity had been erased. A lifetime had been dissolved.

# George, a Man with Old Values Still in Practice

He came down the road, jaunty and erect. The polished walking stick he used marched along beside him like a soldier. When he saw me in the yard, he turned into the driveway. At the fence he stopped and introduced himself. That was the first time I met our neighbor George.

He became more than a fine friend and a neighbor. He became an experience. He was all the old values still in practice. George had endured hardships with grace. He hadn't soured, he had seasoned.

He was born in Poland a few years after the turn of the century to parents who enjoyed wealth and status. But the lines shift quickly in Poland.

It has been a battleground for Europe since the first ancient tribes lifted their clubs against each other, and it was no different in World War I. When it ended his family had plenty of bitter memories and not much else. They had become victims of the Bolshevik Revolution, which had chewed up part of Poland.

They persevered, however, and George received a degree in agricultural chemistry from the University of Warsaw. He became a captain in the Polish Army, and when the Germans attacked in 1939 he was on the front. When Poland fell he was captured. For five years he was a prisoner of war.

The Germans devastated Poland. When they began retreating before the Russians, they destroyed Warsaw. And the Russians delayed their advance so the Germans could crush the Polish patriots who thought the Russians had come to liberate them. But the Russians knew the patriots would resist them as doggedly as they had the Germans, said George, and they wanted them out of the way before they saddled Poland with a Communist dictatorship. The Russians made a realist out of him, and his hatred for them was cold and abiding.

When World War II ended, Poland fell to the Russians and George made it to England with his family. From there he migrated to the United States. The sponsor he had to have before he could enter the country owned a large Texas ranch that he hired George to manage.

After several years, he became dissatisfied with Texas ranch life and moved with his family to California. While he worked full time in a wood-working shop, he studied for a degree in rubber chemistry. When he retired from the rubber company he started working for after he had completed his education, George moved to Oregon and settled upon a 10 acre place near ours.

George was an American citizen, and he worried about the United States. He was afraid the country was going soft. The Russians had a saying he often repeated to describe the American plight. "It will get so good it will kill you," he would say. Deep down, I think he was suspicious of luxury.

He was an American, but first he was a Pole. He yearned for his homeland. He talked about how it was when he was young. And always he remembered the good things: The good food, the wines, the dances. It all shimmered with an aura of romance, which the past has the power to cast upon our memories.

He was Catholic. When the weather was nice, he walked by our place with his wife on their way to church. She was a slender, intense Polish woman with burning dark eyes, who had borne her share of troubles. One morning George went by alone, and I asked him where she was. "The little one has lost faith," he said. "She has seen too much."

And I remembered her talking about the morning she had heard shooting in the rural Polish village where she lived during World War II. It was coming from the Jewish settlement which was all ablaze. As she watched, German soldiers shot the Jews as they ran from their burning homes. Sometimes, faith asks more than one can give.

After that, I got the feeling that going to church was just a chance for George to exercise. One afternoon, as we were fixing a fence, I asked him if he believed in God. He straightened up and swung his arm in a slow half circle. "There is God," he said, "in the trees, the mountains, the sky. God is everywhere, but not often in the heart of man."

George is dead. His ashes were mixed with a bottle of Polish soil he had brought with him years before. They were returned to Poland where they were interred.

He is home now. In spirit he stands beside the Poles who are standing firm against Russia today. He is home now in a land he never ever really left.

# Taking It the Way It Comes

It was a drizzly gray day, sort of chilly, one of those draggy winter days that don't seem to be designed for any particular purpose, except to keep time moving.

When noon finally rolled around I pulled into a little cafe I had passed earlier. It wasn't fancy. The rich didn't gather there to hobnob over caviar, but it was clean and neat.

I took a stool next to an old guy with a fine mustache twirled tightly at each end, and a head of dignified white hair. His clothes were a little on the shabby side, but he looked dapper.

That's the way some people are. A certain grace is natural to them. A certain careless gentility. Clothes don't make them, they make the clothes. That's the kind he was.

He glanced up from the bowl of soup he was eating as I sat down. "Better try some of this," he said. "It's hot enough to keep you warm for a month."

He spoke with such authority I took his advice. And as I waited for my order I asked if he was traveling.

He shook his head. "I live down the road a couple of blocks," he said, "in an old barn of a house that's been there since the year one. It isn't much, but I like it 'cause it's cheap."

"You on social security?" I asked.

"Yeah," he said, "what there is of it."

He had worked as a maintenance man for a big company in

Portland for 35 years. Just before he retired his wife had died, and he didn't want to stick around where so many memories waited to haunt him.

That's the reason he was there. And he wasn't objecting any because it was cheaper to live in a little town. "Every little bit helps," he said.

Most of the time he fixed his own meals, he said, but once in a while he splurged. I had caught him in the middle of a binge. He grinned as he shoved his empty bowl toward the edge of the counter.

In the summer, he said, it was a snap, but the winters sometimes got a little too long to suit his tastes. He lit a cigarette to go with his coffee, and slowly snuffed the match out in the ash tray.

"Trouble is," he said, "we go through life never knowing what we need to know. We believe everything everyone tells us and think we should have everything they say we need. But when you stop and look at it, getting by can be pretty simple."

The old house he lived in had an oil furnace, but he never turned it on. "No sir," he said. "I got an electric heater in the bathroom I can turn on when I'm going to shave or take a bath, but that's all. I can't afford to burn oil."

"But how do you stay warm?"

"I put on more clothes."

"And you stay healthy?"

"I feel better than I've felt in a long time. After you get used to it you don't even notice."

When I suggested that he see about getting some sort of assistace, he shook his head disgustedly. "That's the trouble already," he said, "too many people running around with their hands out looking for a free ride."

He was an admirable old man: proud, independent and self-sufficient. But it really didn't make much sense. While politicians were splashing American millions around the world he was feasting on a bowl of soup and living in a house he couldn't afford to heat.

# The Things that Count

I had never heard of Mr. Loop until he called. I'm glad he did. He was a rare one — one of the few.

His voice was strained and wheezy over the phone, and hard to understand. But finally he got his message across: he wanted to talk to me about selling his personal property at auction because he and his wife were leaving the state.

They lived in a small, neat stucco house at the end of a narrow gravelled road, where a giant grove of oak trees stood. Over the phone he had told me they had sold the small acreage they owned there.

My knock was answered by a small, quiet, dignified woman whose dark hair was frosted with age. When I asked to see Mr. Loop she led me into the dining room where he was stretched out in a reclining chair. As he straightened up, he motioned for me to sit down.

"What's your trouble?" I asked.

"Cancer," he said, "and tuberculosis and a few other things that don't amount to a damn."

The exertion of raising up had cost him, and while he gasped for breath I sipped coffee his wife had served in a cup and saucer decorated with dark blue willows.

"Want to sell out," he said finally, "and go to Washington."

"Why Washington?"

"Going to Bellingham to die."

"You're not old enough to cash in your chips yet."

"If I'm not old enough at 84," he said, "I'm going to be leaving the party early." Then he grinned, the way good losers do.

We talked for a while, and when I asked him if I could take a look at livestock and equipment he wanted to sell, he nodded. And he would go along, just to keep me "honest."

"But you'll have to take it slow," he said. "I don't move as fast as I used to."

It took us a while to reach the barn because he had to stop often and catch his breath. On the way, he told me that his wife, Sally, had relatives in Bellingham and he wanted her near them when he checked out. He knew his days were numbered, he said, and he wanted to make sure she was taken care of.

We agreed to the terms of the sale, and I told him I would be back to get things in order. When I left, he was sitting on the steps of the porch, wheezing for breath.

In a few days I went back with another fellow to get set up for the auction. I stopped by the house to tell them what we were there for, and Mr. Loop said he would be out after a while. Before long, he shuffled up and sat down on an old wheelbarrow to watch us work.

"You fellows won't get nothing done," he said finally. "You don't cuss enough."

I don't remember how much cussing we did, but we finally finished. And then we all sat on the porch and drank lemonade his wife had fixed as late afternoon shadows stretched out across the yard.

It was a nice day for the sale, and under the old oaks it was cool and shady. Since Mr. Loop wanted to see what was going on, we moved an ancient leather sofa out under the trees so he could lie down.

When I started the familiar old spiel about how they were leaving the state, and how I figured their leaving was the community's loss — which I really did — Mrs. Loop moved over beside her husband.

As I talked on, she began to cry and Mr. Loop reached out and took her hand in both of his. I saw a lot of things while I was in the auction business, but that was the most touching of all: two old people holding to each other as their world started coming apart.

After the sale was over, and we had finished settling up, Mr. Loop motioned for me to follow him as he shuffled off to the bedroom. When he had closed the door, he got down on his knees in front of a box packed with blankets and rummaged around until he came up with a bottle of whisky.

"This is only for special occasions," he said as he unscrewed the cap.

When I handed it back, he took a small sip, then stared across the room with the bottle resting on the floor between his knees.

"Now," he said quietly, "Sally will have someone to look after her when I'm gone."

Before he put it away, he raised the bottle up to the window to see how much was left. "But I ain't going till that's gone," he said. As he slipped the bottle back into the box, he grinned.

I got one Christmas card from them after they moved to Bellingham. When none came the next year I assumed Mr. Loop had died. But he was ready, and I'll bet he checked out without a whimper.

When my number comes up, I hope to do as well.

# Winners that Lose

Phil was about six feet tall, broad-shouldered and well built. His face was square and strong. He had black curly hair, and a dark tan that made his eyes seem bluer than they were. He was a good looking guy.

He was a brother of my sister's girlfriend and he was going to stay with my folks for awhile. World War II had just ended, and he was sort of drifting around until he got his feet back on the ground. He wasn't looking for money, he said. He just wanted a place to stay, and he was willing to work for that.

For about a week things rocked along really smooth. Phil fitted right in. Before long he was a member of the family. He was eager to help, and he had an easy laugh that didn't take much nudging. I think my folks were hoping that some of his ways would rub off on my brother and me.

It was June, and Phil had helped haul hay that morning. It was rather warm, but it wasn't hot. We had washed up for dinner at a faucet in the yard because we were pretty dirty. After he had splashed water on his hands and face, Phil dried them on a towel Mother had sent out.

When he was through he stood there waiting for the rest of us to finish. I thought he looked a little strange when he handed me the towel, but I didn't give it a second thought. I figured water in my eyes was distorting my vision.

We had started for the house when Phil's knees went limp and he began staggering like a drunk. A strange look slipped into his eyes.

Quizzical surprise is the only term I can find to describe it. When he went down he flopped over on his back and his eyes rolled up in his head. He began shaking violently and every muscle in his body strained as though they were going to pull in two. We didn't know what to do. After we had put a cold cloth on his forehead, he started coming around. We thought he'd had a heat stroke. But he hadn't.

He had been wounded in the Army, and a shell fragment had been removed from his head. Because it had been damaged beyond repair, part of his skull had been replaced with a metal plate. The way it was explained to us, the seizures occurred when Phil got too warm. His sister said nothing could be done to help him. After they had run their course, she said he would be okay for a while. But they left him pretty shaky. They took a lot out of him.

Our neighbor ran a hatchery. She was an older woman, small, but strong and confident. She said she would give Phil a job if he wanted to work for her. His condition didn't bother her, she said. She didn't think they would have any trouble.

She came to get Phil about noon one day. She drove a station wagon, and after he had put his stuff in the back he crawled in the front seat beside her. As he closed the door that strange look came swimming into his eyes again and he slumped over against Mrs. Smith. As he went into convulsions his body wedged in between hers and the steering wheel. When his hands tightened around the wheel it seemed that he was going to pull it right up through the floorboards.

Mrs. Smith didn't panic. She stayed cool. She sat very still until Phil's seizure had passed, then she said, "Perhaps I had better make other arrangements."

Phil was getting a disability pension. He needed one because he couldn't hold a job. He tried, but he disturbed people. Finally he went to a veteran's hospital. That's where he was the last time I saw him. He was sitting on a bench in the shade of an old oak tree, staring out across the green, grassy grounds. Since I had seen him last, a vacant emptiness had crowded everything else out of his eyes.

He was living in some strange, shadowy world because the life he could have led had fizzled out through a hole in his head. And I find that rather ironical because our side had won the war. Phil was one of the victors. Wasn't he?

# Trying to Get a Handle
# on the Past

It was a chill, drizzly morning and he was standing on the approach to the freeway. I noticed the light vest he wore as he raised his thumb.

He thanked me for stopping as he crawled in and crowded a suitcase into the seat between us. Then he leaned over his knees and shivered.

He was about frozen, he said. He had spent five hours the night before trying to hitch a ride that never came by. At two in the morning he had given up. In a clump of trees across the freeway he had huddled up until it started getting light.

He was an older fellow. Later he would tell me that he was 60, but all he could do for a while was shiver and shake. With a nod of genuine appreciation he took the coffee I offered him.

His face was weathered and worn, like a piece of old canvas that had been left outside too long. As he sat there staring straight ahead, it looked like a painting of patient sadness.

He was heading for Tempe, Arizona, he said, to see his son who was going to the university there. His son didn't know he was coming. He probably wouldn't have recognized him anyway. They had been separated for 20 years.

He and his wife had divorced shortly after their son was born, he said, and he had lost track of him. But a few days before he had met a relative in Seattle who told him that he was going to school in Arizona. He didn't know how big Tempe was. "But it's just outside Phoenix," he said.

If he'd had the money he wouldn't have been hitchhiking. He

didn't enjoy it. It was too risky. In Washington where he lived two hitchhikers had been murdered. He was worried. He never knew, he said, when he got in a car what condition he would be in when he got out.

He kept watching the sky. Patches of blue could occasionally be seen through the gray, slow-shifting clouds. He was hoping for fair weather. He didn't have the clothes to be traveling in the cold. The day before he had left his coat lying in the back of a car he had been given a ride in. For more than an hour he waited because he thought the driver might bring it back.

Losing the coat was bad enough. What made it worse was the loss of the nitroglycerine pills that were in one of the pockets. He needed them for his heart, which was still weak from an attack he had suffered two years ago. His doctor had told him he was crazy to start out on such a wild goose chase. He smiled wearily. He was about ready to agree with him.

He looked beat. When I said so, he nodded. But he would be okay if the weather held, he said. Somewhere down the line he would find a place where he could lie down for a while.

He had logged and fished commercially. He said he had perfected a portable, chain-saw sawmill that was superior to anything on the market. A prototype he'd build had performed even better than he had expected. As soon as he got some money ahead he was going to advertise it. "When you get in my shape," he said, "you got to come up with a scheme."

A "magnetic engine" was one scheme he had worked on for years. When he got it perfected, he said it would "run between 5,000 and 6,000 miles on one charge of two 12-volt batteries." I didn't ask him about it. It seemed to make even sadder the plight he was in.

I asked him why it was important after all these years to see a son he wouldn't even recognize. He didn't know. Not really. But he knew it was.

When I turned off he eased out of the car. "I get up kind of slow," he said with an apologetic smile. Then he started walking slowly down the freeway, an old man with an illusion about reaching back across all those years and making everything come out right again.

# An Odd Couple
# in an Ancient House

It was an ancient, two-story house, long and tall and narrow. It sat on a quiet, shaded street, a dark brown ghostly relic from the past. With gingerbread around the eaves, it maintained an illusion of its former grandeur, but it definitely was an illusion.

For about a year I lived there, if lived is the proper word. Just off the hall I rented one room with two tall, slim windows that looked as though they were trying to hide something.

It was a high-ceilinged room with a sink hanging from the wall and a two-burner hot plate standing beside it on a loose-legged table. Next to the hot plate was an old cupboard that could be closed off with a square of cloth that slid on a string.

It was heated with wood that had to be carried from a shed at the rear of the house. I still don't know what the landlord had in mind when he installed the stove. It put out more heat than an infected thumb. If it had been perched on the North Pole, it would have melted all the snow within 20 miles. It was that big.

I guess that's the reason I never took to saunas. By the time they came into vogue, that stove had sweated the desire right out of me. I always figured the heat it created had caused the big blue, flowery blisters in the paper that covered the walls.

It had been a fine old house in its day, but its day had long passed by the time I got there. By then it had been a boarding house for years and it had attracted some strange people, who appreciated the low rent as much as I did.

Upstairs there were three rented rooms and a community bath. Downstairs there was my room, plus the one Zeke and Millie occupied across the hall.

They were one of the weirdest pairs I've ever seen. They provided variety of the most unexpected kind.

He was short, with a small, bashed-in face like ham-and-egg fighters usually wind up with. She was big, with a pale face round as the moon and eyes clear and blue as a gas flame. They were in their 40's and they drank like fish.

Zeke drew a pension for some kind of medical disability and Millie worked as a waitress when they ran low on booze, which caused them some dandy problems. When they drank, all the old grievances floated to the surface, and they would tear into each other like a pair of tigers. They could be heard for miles.

In the middle of one hot summer night, they woke me up. Millie had apparently discovered some very unsavory something in Zeke's past, and she was letting him have it with both barrels. She was in the middle of a long, muddled harangue when the door to my room flew open.

It was Zeke, seeking refuge. As he slammed the door, I could see him staggering like a shadow through the gloom. It had happened before. Once I had tried to lock him out, but he had pounded on the door so hard he had awakened everyone in the house.

I crawled out of bed. Sleep was out of the question, and I didn't want to listen to his tale of woe for the 100th time. I told him I was going out and curl up in the car. And I didn't really mind. I figured it would be cooler out there anyway.

I woke up in the seat, stiff and cramped. Dawn was pushing a pale gray light over the horizon, and I got out and trudged up the steps. The door to their room was open, and I closed it quietly. I didn't want to get them started again.

Wearily I opened my door and stepped inside. And there they were, sleeping peacefully in my bed. They were a picture of marital bliss, which shattered one of my cherished beliefs.

If you make your own bed, says the old adage, you must lie in it. If that's true, how come Zeke and Millie wound up in mine?

# Of Strong Fathers
# and Weak Sons

When I met him he was a big old man with square shoulders and a slow, determined way of walking. His eyes were steady, and his face was seamy with wrinkles. It had weathered well in the outdoors where he had spent most of his life.

By working hard and hanging in there when most everyone else had pulled out, he had managed to accumulate several thousand acres which he turned into a ranch where whiteface cattle ran. He was a good cowman and he prospered.

He also had accumulated a wife and three sons. I don't know where they got it because the old man wasn't that way, nor was their mother, but the boys were a reckless bunch. As most reckless people are, they were carefree. They didn't worry about the consequences of their actions. I guess old Sam had instilled in them the idea that he could handle whatever happened.

And he gave that impression. He was authority well packaged in a solid six-foot frame. He didn't try to impose his presence, but everyone was aware of it. He was endowed with that certain something that make people take a second look. He was noticed wherever he went.

The boys seemed to enjoy what they were doing. As far as I know, they got along well. Old Sam had bailed them out of a couple of scrapes for drinking and fighting, but it was nothing serious.

Then he died. He was in his 70's, but the boys were still in their 20's because he had married late in life, and almost immediately things started coming unglued.

113

The old man had been a steadying influence. He was one of those rare individuals who governed without seeming to do so. When he bowed out the boys were lost. They were rootless. They didn't know how to handle responsibility, and they went wilder than pet coons.

It didn't take them long to go through the cattle and then the ranch. Within three years it was all gone, despite the tearful pleas of their mother. And about all they had to show for it were some scars picked up in barroom brawls.

I'm sure old Sam must have turned over in his grave a dozen times as they tore through the ranch he had worked so hard to create. It almost seemed as though the boys were getting even with him for leaving them in the lurch.

Maybe they were. The bond that exists between fathers and sons is snarled and knotted in ways hard to understand. And it's ironic. And sad, too, the way a man's dream is sometimes destroyed by the ones he wanted most to share it with.

But it's not as sad as the son who tries to be the man his father wants him to be, when he's not cut out to be that kind of man. That was the bind Junior found himself in.

His dad owned a construction outfit I once worked for. He was a rugged, red-faced individualist who knew what he wanted and didn't hesitate to fight for it.

Junior was made of different stuff. He wasn't the type for that hard-driving, hard-drinking business, but the old man did his best to make him fit.

Poor Junior. He had no one's respect. Even though he was well educated and knew the business, he was treated with indifference by everyone. You don't make friends and influence people on a construction job by standing around with a box of pink tissues under your arm because your nose is running from an allergy.

He acted like he was miserable, and I'm sure he was. But not because of the runny nose. He must have been the loneliest person on earth. I'm sure he knew he could never satisfy his dad, and the old man must've known it too.

Dreams are hard to relinquish. And they are powerful concoctions: some people they make, and others they break.

# Hokey, Who Chose Death
# as an Answer

Hokey was big, strong, well-built and healthy. He was in his late 20's and most of his life was still ahead of him the night he stepped out in front of a freight train, which knocked him straight into the life hereafter.

No one understood why he chose that method of departure. Those of us who knew him assumed he was despondent over the loss of Jo, the woman he was living with. It was a rather strange alliance, by any standard.

Jo was blonde. She was nearly as tall as Hokey. She was flat-faced and strong. To say that she was on the masculine side was to put it mildly. In the commonly accepted sense, she was not attractive.

But to Hokey she was something special. She seemed to regard him in the same light. Even though they drank a lot, no one ever heard them fight. They seemed one of the best matched couples around.

Then one day Hokey showed up at the bar alone. He was never much of a talker, and that day he had even less to say. Actually, he was a loner. Except for Jo, he didn't associate with anyone. After that, he was seen alone more and more.

He became edgy, and his eyes smouldered. They became sullen, and people left him alone. He was hurting pretty bad, but he wouldn't let anyone get close. There was speculation that he would go off his rocker if something didn't happen. And Jo was no help. She had left town.

No one really expressed much sympathy, or surprise for that matter, when they scraped Hokey off the cow catcher of that loco-

115

motive. There was evidence that he had been drinking, according to the officials. And I heard that a search of next of kin proved fruitless.

Jo made his life worthwhile. There seemed to be no other conclusion. As long as she was there, he had something to revolve around. When she left, he swung out of orbit. His mind must have looped around wildly looking for something to replace her. Obviously, it failed to find anything.

Since he wasn't one to talk about his feelings, I have no idea what his values were. I often wonder. I often wonder what was going through his mind when he stepped out in front of that train. Whatever it was, it was compelling. To keep your feet from running when a railroad engine is coming down on you takes something pretty powerful.

I guess what makes it strange was Hokey's appearance. His face was square, his jaw firm. His eyes were direct. He didn't look like the kind that would run from anything. Even if he were scared, you figured he would hang in there until the last dog was hung. That was the impression he gave.

But looks are so deceptive. We are all so vulnerable. We look for something that will prove our worth, our identity. Among friends we find it, and the things we accomplish. We go through our motions day by day knowing — sometimes mistakenly — that someone somewhere cares.

Only when I think of life in those terms can I begin to feel the isolation that Hokey must have experienced after Jo pulled out. Apparently she was the scale by which he judged his values. When she left, he must have decided he wasn't worthy of the space he was taking up on the face of this strange earth we share.

He committed suicide. That was the legal verdict. Those who are supposed to know denounce suicide as an irrational act. It may well be. And it may be morally wrong. I don't know. But suicide is not an illogical act.

It is a solution to a problem. And a solution was what Hokey was looking for the night he stepped out in front of that train. I hope he wasn't judged too harshly.

# Rewards are
# Where You Find Them

I was lost. I hadn't been able to locate the party I had spent most of the afternoon looking for. I decided I would follow the narrow, winding road I was on a little further before I gave up. Then I could say in good conscience that I had exhausted all the possibilities.

It was late afternoon, and shade from the trees that grew beside the road darkened it in shadows. After a while I began feeling uneasy, as though I was being watched by someone who resented my intrusion.

The stillness, the absence of any movement, intensified that feeling, as did the silence that thrummed in my ears when I stopped to drink from a small stream trickling down a draw.

Then the road suddenly ran out. It ended in a small, sun-splashed clearing, where a small cabin stood. In surprise I sat there looking at it. It was unpainted, and it had weathered a soft brown color that matched the wooden picket fence that surrounded it.

As I stepped out of the car an old black and tan hound lying on the porch raised its head and thumped the floor with his tail a couple of times. It wasn't the place I was looking for, that was for sure.

Before I reached the door I heard the sound of metal hitting metal behind the house. From the end of the porch, I could see an old flat bed truck standing at the edge of the timber, next to a shed that had been recently built of rough, raw lumber.

No one answered my knock on the door, and the old hound roused himself and trailed along as I started for the shed. The unease that had twinged my mind earlier was still working on my imagination as I crossed the yard.

He was in his late 60's. He had a square rugged face, thick white hair and dark blue eyes. He was thick through the shoulders. His hands were big and his arms bulged with muscles. When I walked in he was setting a jack under a big, yellow diesel engine that was pointing toward a bunch of machinery piled up at one end of the shed.

He grinned and nodded as he stood up and wiped his hands on a rag he stuffed back in his hip pocket when he was through. No sir, he didn't know anyone by the name of the party I was looking for, he said, as he introduced himself.

But he was happy to have someone come along. Got kind of lonely living there alone, he told me. Not that he lacked something to do. He had some timber he was going to cut into lumber as soon as he got his sawmill set up.

He was working alone, and I was amazed at what he had done in less than a year. From outside where it had been unloaded, he had moved his diesel engine into the shed with jacks, come-a-longs and pry bars. By hand he had mixed concrete and poured piers halfway down the side of the building where it was going to sit. He still had about 50 feet to go, and he figured he would have it where he wanted it in a week or so.

For him it was a dream come true. He was a retired logger, and for years he had planned on supplementing his income with lumber cut from his own logs. He guessed he could have hired some help, but he didn't need any. It was his project. Since his wife died he needed something to keep him busy. He needed to be tired enough so he could sleep when he went to bed.

"All I got to worry about," he said, "is me and old Bozo." Stretched out in the sun near the door, old Bozo seemed quite content with that arrangement.

When I left it was nearly dark. He invited me to stay for supper, and I wish I could have. As I drove back down that narrow, winding road I thought about the unease that had been preying upon my mind as I approached the shed.

Then I thought about the pleasant, unexpected way life sometimes rewards us when we are expecting the worst. And how it sometimes pays to go to the end of the road.

# A MIXED BAG

# What Fun to Weather the Storm

I think it was Mark Twain who was supposed to have said, "Everyone talks about the weather, but no one does anything about it."

We're lucky, I think, that no one does. A shot of quirky weather now and then keeps us on our toes. Without it our lives would get stale as a gale without a wind. It creates all sorts of interesting situations.

A couple of years ago it had rained more than usual, if that's possible in Oregon, and a big, droopy fellow, pale and pallid from too long spent under a sunless sky, dropped anchor beside me as I waited on a downtown corner for the light to change. As he watched the rain explode around us like a jillion tiny shellbursts, he soggily shook his head.

"If things don't change pretty quick," he said, "I'm going to get out of here even if I have to hijack a plane."

It sounded like a good idea to me, and I supported it wholeheartedly. To prove it, I told him I would loan him a water pistol if I had one handy, so he wouldn't have to worry about running short of ammunition. He nodded his thanks as he splashed off toward the airport. I haven't seen him since.

Instead of waking up to a cold and gloomy morning filled with fog and frost, think about rising in a land where the sun comes up bright and cheery every day. And think how it would affect one who is by nature glum and pessimistic, whose greatest pleasure is watching a car careen down a frosty street with the driver frozen behind the wheel as it grazes a telephone pole and spins into the intersection the way a Tempest, a Comet or a Fury should. What fun. What a glorious way to start a day.

And think what would happen to our conversation if the weather didn't act up once in a while. Rain will perk it up most of the time, and fog and frost will usually carry it over soggy spots. But it takes sleet, snow and ice to really make it sparkle.

Any one of them will add zest, but when all three are present at once, the very air begins to throb and vibrate to the choicest expletives this side of the Belgian Congo.

Which makes me wonder if people who live in warm and tropical climates ever develop a first class inventory of cuss words. I doubt it. If they've never had to put chains on in a wind-whipped storm, they probably never needed one.

I suppose it would be a flagrant waste to use profanity in a climate where the danger of drowning in a tall glass of spirited water is the greatest threat to a long and torpid life. No doubt about it, cursing is the rightful nomenclature of blizzards and storms, frosted fingers and frozen toes.

Once in Wyoming I met a fellow who had been sorely deprived as a child. He had been raised somewhere — and I can't imagine such a place — where it never snowed. The only kind he'd seen was the warm, white, fluffy stuff that settles with such pretty precision on the pages of Family Circle at Christmas time.

It was understandable then that he should be overcome with rapture when it began to snow that fall. In a fit of ecstasy he bleated words like "beautiful" and "gorgeous" and "bedecked." I'm sure he got around to the "heavenlies," the "sublimes" and the "divines" before he was through. He was headed in that direction when I left. But all good things come to an end.

When I saw him three months later, he was sitting in a small, steamy restaurant where the chili was so hot it would singe an arctic wind. As he gingerly stirred a bowl of that liquified fire, he stared hypnotically out the window at the falling snow.

"That goddam white stuff is still coming down," he said in a soft, disbelieving voice.

Should anything that can stimulate such profundity be changed? I don't think so. Without the weather our lives would become like floods without water, like lightning without fire — all thunder and no roar.

# Monotonous Jobs Give Perspective to Life

Sometimes when I lose sight of the good things in life, I take a look back at some of the monotonous, grinding jobs I've had. I think it is important that everybody have a few in their past.

They provide perspective. For those who have never held such jobs I feel a special pity. Never will they know the joy that comes at quitting time.

Poking wires on an old stationary hay baler is the kind of job I'm talking about. How enjoyable it was when the temperature soared to 100 degrees in the shade, and the only shade was a cloud of dust hovering overhead.

If there was a dirtier job I've yet to hear about it. And if you didn't get the wires poked through so the kid on the other side of the baler could tie them, the bales wouldn't come out looking like bales at all and someone was sure to be unhappy.

It made no difference how you dressed. Six handkerchiefs and a bed sheet knotted tightly around your neck wouldn't keep the dust and dirt out. Your lungs were treated to a dust storm every time you breathed, and after a couple of hours you were so begrimed you could pass in the night without being seen.

The only things I remember about poking wires was the walk to the river at the end of the day. But the river probably didn't look forward to seeing us. As soon as we dove into that cool, clear water it looked like it had been dyed dark brown.

We were walking erosion and water pollution all silted into grimy, red-eyed phantoms. If the Department of Environmental Quality had been around we would have been outlawed.

But that's not the only job I remember so un-fondly. An old well I helped clean out ranks right up there with it. If it had been filled with dirt, it wouldn't have been so bad. But it contained many other things.

Old tin cans were there in abundance. So were bottles, the kind used for distilled spirits. From the number we discovered I concluded that whoever filled the well had done so for their own preservation.

A hole in the ground would certainly have been a threat to their long lives if they had come stumbling around after inhaling the contents of all those empty bottles.

It was deep, too. We reached 30 feet and still hadn't found water. We wondered if we ever would. After five more feet of digging, our wondering came to an end. We had arrived at the bottom of a dry hole. Unless we could squeeze some moisture out of it, we had done a lot of dirty work for nothing.

So we dug a little deeper and stuck in four or five sticks of dynamite to see if we could jar something loose. And we did. All the dirt we blew up made it a lot easier to fill the hole back up again.

But that job wasn't without rewards. As a result of it I found out I didn't know a well from a hole in the ground. That isn't much consolation, but when you've dug that deep for water that wasn't there you're grateful for anything you can dredge up.

Those weren't the best of jobs, but they weren't the worst I ever had. Stacking lumber for a dry kiln holds that distinction. All day long it was 2 x 4's, 2 x 6's, and great thick 2 x 12 slabs of boredom.

On low flat cars that ran on rails we stacked them about eight feet high. Between each layer we put spacers so the lumber would dry uniformly as heat in the kiln circulated through the cracks. Over and over we did that — day after day.

But we did get a break occasionally. When the loads had dried we got to re-stack the lumber we had stacked two or three days before. It was like greeting old friends over and over. And it's surprising how boring they can get when met so often even under such stimulating circumstances.

That kind of job does something to you after a while. When the jitney driver pulled up with another load of lumber to be stacked, I would often ask myself this question: If someone clobbered him with a 2 x 4 and there was no one around to hear him yell, would there be any sound? Jobs like that can become a menace to society.

Karl Marx, who blessed the world with communism, claimed that workers become alienated from their jobs when they could no longer see the result of their labor.

I don't see anything so profound about that statement. I could've told him that. But I'm not going to argue the point. I just hope I'm so alienated from some of the jobs I've had I'll never see the results again.

# Drawing from Experience

Draftsmen who illustrate mechanical manuals and books on building have it down pat. I envy them. Everything works out the way it's supposed to when they do things.

Every board in every building they lay out on paper fits perfectly. They never run into snags when they begin overhauling a piece of machinery. They never have trouble with rusty bolts. And all the holes line up so neat and clean.

I wish they had drawn a diagram for us when a neighbor and I began roofing our barn. It had a steep roof I'd stripped with 2 x 4's so there would be something to nail the metal to. Until we got to the end we walked on them. Then we nailed a cleat along the bottom edge of the roof, which supported the ladder we climbed while we hammered the last piece of metal into place.

All went well until we tried to take the cleat off. The nails had seized and it wouldn't budge. They have to be pulled from a ladder, and it yawed around most uncomfortably when we reefed hard on a crowbar.

Finally, Charlie shook his head. "That's the story of my life," he said. "There's always one nail that won't pull, or one nut that won't come loose."

All those beautiful, balanced symmetrical lines draftsmen draw to show us how simple the most complex thing can be swam through my mind when he said that. Had they been doing it, that cleat would have come off like a work of art.

In one of their illustrations those nails would have come out of that knotty old board with halos around their shiny heads. In fact, they would probably have been so eager to help they wouldn't have allowed themselves to be driven in the first place.

I've often wondered how they would have portrayed a dramatic little scene I witnessed one afternoon while helping Rick and his dad tear down an old granary.

It was a high-ball job. Rick, who was a lean, quick and nervous guy in his late 30's, liked to see things happen. He didn't have time for delays.

His dad was in his 70's and he didn't move very fast. But Rick didn't say anything until the old man took what Rick considered too long knocking down a rafter that was resisting him with all its splintery might.

"Here," he said, as he stepped in front of him, "I'll get that S.O.B."

When he jerked his arm back over his shoulder the claws of the hammer caught the old man in the center of the forehead. There immediately followed one of the richest mixtures of blood and profanity that eyes have seen or ears have heard.

The old man threw his hammer and it thunked angrily into the wall on the opposite side of the granary. "Damned if I'll work with an idiot like that," he announced loudly as he whipped a big blue bandanna out of his overalls and plastered it against his forehead.

Nothing of that sort would have happened if an illustrator had been dismantling that building on paper. There wouldn't have been any dust or dirt, I know. The sun wouldn't have been glaring like a hot tin dish, either. And there wouldn't have been any nails to step on. It would have been as neat and clean as a toothpaste ad.

With one sweeping swing of his hammer Rick would have knocked that rafter loose, and there wouldn't have been any of that screeching sound old nails make when they're being pulled. And his dad wouldn't have got busted in the head.

Even if that couldn't have been avoided, I'm sure it wouldn't have produced the same result. A good illustrator could have made it look like getting hit in the head with a hammer was a normal, natural occurrence required occasionally to clear one's sinuses. And the old man would have rewarded Rick with a grateful smile, no doubt.

It certainly would have looked a lot prettier, there's no doubt about it. But it couldn't have compared to the real thing. When a nail won't pull, and someone flies off the handle, it's a lot more exciting.

# A Time to Stand
# and a Time to Fall

As I drove back and forth from work each day, I admired the building the two men were putting up beside the road. That's the nice thing about carpentry work. At the end of every day you can usually see what someone else has accomplished.

It was going to be a long, narrow building. A machine shop, I decided, or a shop. And the two fellows were doing a nice job. It looked like they were being a little Scotch with their bracing, but I didn't give it much thought. From the job they were doing, I figured they knew what they were about.

They had completed the walls, and one evening as I came home they were starting to put up the rafters. But that night a big wind came up and the next morning when I went to work the building that had almost been was a pile of rubble scattered all over the ground.

I wish I had been there when they walked out to find their building a wreck. On second thought, I'm glad I wasn't. I don't like to hear the screech of nails being pulled before their time has come. And when grown men cry, I believe they should be left alone.

Slowly the building took shape again. And it was certainly well braced the second time it went up. Whoever said that experience is the best teacher certainly hit the nail squarely on the head.

Not long ago I watched another building go up beside the road. It was a tall, barn-like structure. It sat farther back from the road than the first one, but even at a distance it didn't appear that it had enough bracing. But I'm no expert, so I decided to wait and see. I hoped I was wrong. It was a nice building.

But the wind that came huffing and puffing out of the hills one night was no respecter of nice buildings and blew it to smithereens. Such a waste of time and labor. But the builders apparently had an ample supply of profanity to tide them over the initial shock. Since then the building has risen again. A much sturdier building, I might add.

We didn't have such good luck with one we built. It was a double garage that someone had designed for my dad. Maybe he designed it, I don't remember. It could have been me, but I hope not.

It turned out that we had a little trouble with bracing, also. But we were spared any wind during the construction phase, so we had no trouble finishing it. Since the front was wide open it should have been strengthened with braces nailed diagonally across the ceiling joints. I think we slapped in a couple short ones and called it good.

It wasn't. The first big wind that came along didn't take it down, but the next morning it sure had a knock-kneed appearance. Before it completely gave up the ghost, we set out to straighten it up. With the blade on a crawler tractor we started realigning things, which is about like trying to dust fine china with a broom. If we pushed one place, it bulged in another. If we tried to pull instead of push, the bulges reversed and became blisters on the other side.

We fiddled around for nearly a day before we concluded that we had accomplished as much as we were going to, which wasn't much. Despite our efforts, it still looked like a building suffering from a ruptured equilibrium. We tried not to look as we picked up our tools. That may have been the problem.

As I drove the tractor out of the garage, where I had been using the blade to line up the sill on the foundation, the chain fastened to the drawbar somehow hooked the end of the wall. I couldn't have imagined anything like that happening in my wildest dreams, and I wasn't prepared to make a quick stop when I heard the tortured sound of lumber being reduced to splinters.

What the wind hadn't been able to do, I did in much less time. And after I had pulled the wall completely off the foundation, the rest was easy. With just a little help the building collapsed. It never rose again.

The moral to all of that is this: Never complete a building that's going to fall before it's finished. Or something like that.

# Good Times and Bad Times

Have you ever stopped to think about all the times in your life: the good times and bad times, the big times and small times, the hot and cold times?

I don't often, but the arrival of a New Year makes me conscious of time and its passing. For those who had an uproarious New Year's Eve the unconscious passage of time might be more appropriate.

That, of course, leads straight into January, which isn't one of our better times. It's a dismal month, but perhaps it's just as well. After so much holiday gluttony it would be hard to enjoy 30 days of good weather in the goutish disposition we begin the new year with. When she invented the middle of winter, Mother Nature knew what she was doing.

But a mid-winter slump is expected, which more or less eliminates it as a Number 1 bad time. To really take the wind out of your sails, bad times must come unexpectedly.

Take a leaky hot water tank, for example. Until you've awakened one morning to discover that water covering the floor isn't coming from a geothermal well erupting under the house, you'll not realize how unforeseen they can be.

But you'll know by the time you've arrived at the scalding truth how it feels to watch peace and contentment go down the drain. Pray that it happens in winter. Splashing around in warm water isn't quite as depressing when snow is on the ground.

While I'm on the subject of water, I might as well mention pumps, and the many ways they have of going out. They are strange creatures, pumps are. They rarely fail in winter when demand for water is low. They get tired in summer when everything is thirsty. When they lose their prime, you're in for a bad, dried-up time.

So many things come into the world ready made to spoil our pleasure. Tires are one of them — especially tires that go down when they are supposed to stay up.

One that went flat in the Nevada desert 10 miles from nowhere in the middle of the night didn't arouse much joy. And the spare that was flat aroused even less. Walking it 10 miles to the nearest service station for repairs made Mr. Goodyear seem like a whole lot less.

The worst times, it seems to me, are those that come after we've made preparations to avoid them. When I think about them, the wood I stacked inside the shed comes immediately to mind.

I piled it there so it would stay dry. What I failed to notice was the depression on the floor that began filling with water after the winter rains began. There was no trick getting the wood out. It floated well. But it didn't produce the hottest time of my life when we tried to burn it.

But life is not all bad. It comes with an equal amount of good mixed in. Sometimes it takes a little self-deception to detect it, but that's a small price to pay.

It's nice to realize after all those tormented years of watching your hair fall out that baldness is truly a blessing without disguise. It's a time of liberation, actually.

No more combs to buy. No more brushes to worry about. And when you scratch your head you can get right down to business. That, in itself, is worth a lot.

Unlike bad times, the good times we don't anticipate are best. The unexpected makes them better, just as it makes bad times worse.

A good time is discovering a letter in your mailbox that tells you how to win a fortune, instead of finding all the bills you expected. Reader's Digest should be given a medal for all the hopes it has raised with the $200,000 prize money it's promised to pay me for the coupon I've rushed back to get back in the mail.

It hasn't arrived yet, but when it does I'm going to have a big time. I might even have the time of my life — if I've got any left by then.

128

# Indifference is an Easy Thing to Learn

I met him in a Salt Lake City bar. He was a strange guy, handsome, with black curly hair and intense, compelling eyes of color I can't describe. I remember them as colorless, which they surely weren't, but they were different. He talked in a low, confidential voice, as though he didn't want to be overheard.

There were quite a few of us hanging around that bar during late winter. Most of us were killing time, waiting for something to open up so we could go to work. I think he singled me out because I was younger than most of them, which led him to believe I was more gullible. He wasn't wrong.

After he decided I could be trusted, he told me he was from Oklahoma. He had spent a couple of years, he said, for car theft. I didn't pay much attention, but I figured it was for something more serious than that. It could have been anything and I wouldn't have been surprised. He had strange, wild eyes.

He wanted me to go with him to Colorado. He said he knew we could get a job in some kind of fertilizer plant. A friend of his worked there, he said, who could arrange it.

It sounded good to me. I was ready to go. And I would have probably, if he hadn't assured me one night when he was pretty drunk that we wouldn't have to worry about money. As he leaned over the table he reached inside his coat and came up with a snub-nosed .38 caliber pistol. That, it turned out, was the friend he had been talking about.

I shoved back from the table and shook my head. Count me out,

I told him. I want no part of it.

He gave me a long, steady staring look as he slipped the pistol back inside his coat. Then he got up and left. Two mornings later I read about him in a Salt Lake City paper. He had been arrested shortly after shooting up a grocery store he had robbed. He was an escapee from Arkansas, the paper said. He had been serving time for armed robbery.

That happened a long time ago. But a year ago our daughter, Leith, and some of her friends attended a Christian youth convention in Portland. It was a weekend affair, which included a visit to one of the city's largest shopping centers. While there they got to go ice skating in a covered rink, which is a novel experience for one raised in the Northwest where water seldom freezes hard enough to walk on. She and her friends had quite a time, with plenty of falls to keep things interesting.

We live in a rural area, and their exposure to city ways had been limited. Consequently, they were surprised to find other kids at the rink openly selling drugs. They didn't understand why it was being tolerated, since it was against the law.

When the kids selling dope approached them, Leith and her friends complained to the security patrolman, who shrugged and grinned. They were amused by the naivete of such innocent kids.

"It goes on all the time," they said. "No big deal."

"But it's against the law."

"Don't worry about it," they were told. "That's the way it is."

That bothers me. That I did nothing, lo, those many years ago when that guy flashed a pistol also bothers me. It didn't take a genius to know what he was going to do. If I had reported him, someone wouldn't have been robbed and terrified.

But I believe it goes deeper than that. If I had done something then, maybe Leith wouldn't have been harassed by drug dealers in a public place a year ago. If I — and thousands more who didn't want to — had gotten involved, perhaps the crime wave we're putting up with wouldn't be a wave at all.

Indifference isn't cheap, it's just easy.

# AND THE MOOD CHANGES

# March, When the Unexpected Happens

With March comes the wind. And showers mixed with sun. And hail. And sleet. And sometimes snow.

Of all the months, March is the most fickle. It is the month in which the unexpected is expected. It is the warm, sunny morning turned into a rain-soaked afternoon, chill and dreary. It is the rainbow arcing at the foot of the hill on a cloudy day.

March is the month in which desires eternal begin to stir. It's the time for prowling tomcats, and dogs that come dragging home in the early hours after a long night out. March, it appears, awakens the primordial urges. Mysteriously, in some subtle way, it affects the chemistry that percolates among all things living. The effect is sometimes strange indeed.

Take the woodpecker who comes each year to build a nest somewhere in the grove of oak trees that stand between our house and barn. At least that's what I think he comes for. But I wouldn't swear to it, judging from the way he behaves.

I heard him first two years ago, in the early morning while we were still in bed. I wondered on what tree he was hammering to make a sound so loud. I tried to determine where he was as I laid there after he had drummed me wide awake.

I couldn't. But he gave me ample opportunity to find out. He was back the next morning just as day was breaking. It appeared that this was a routine he was in the process of establishing.

As he began warming up, it sounded almost as if he were dinging on a barrel. It had the same hollow, muffled sound. By ignoring him, I thought he might go away. But he didn't like to be ignored. Like a drummer on a binge, he stepped up the tempo.

Finally I got up and sneaked downstairs because I didn't want to scare him before I found out what he was up to. Quietly, I opened the back door and stepped out on the deck. Strange, I thought, that the sound wasn't nearly as loud there as it was upstairs.

I slipped around the corner and searched among the branches of the apple tree that stands beside the house, but he wasn't there. And what he was drumming on didn't really sound like wood. It sounded too tinny for that.

Then I saw him, pounding away on the iron hood that covers our fireplace chimney. No wonder it sounded so loud inside. The sound was rushing down the hollow shaft of the chimney like water through a funnel. And he was enjoying himself no end. I'm convinced he wasn't looking for anything to eat. The satisfaction of pounding out that trip-hammer rhythm was all the satisfaction he was looking for.

I threw a couple of rocks at him, which he ignored. With an old slingshot I found in the barn, I bounced a rock off the hood where he perched. It didn't faze him. He merely shifted around out of sight and rat-a-tatted on. Three more rocks whizzed by his head before he finally decided to call it quits. But every morning he was back.

Now comes March again, and with it our friend the flicker. For the last few mornings he's been rehearsing his staccato solo. On one occasion it sounded different. The pitch was higher. And when I got up to drive him off, I found him whanging on the TV antenna.

I guess after all the years of practice he figures it's time to get some national exposure. I'll have to admit his act is superior to most of the stuff that passes through the boob-tube as entertainment.

He's screwy, there's no doubt of that. I'm not surprised. Anything can happen in March. But soon it will be over and our friend usually hammers enough sense into his head by April to settle for something nice and soft, like an old oak tree.

# Spring

Each dawn lights a new world in the spring. It is a time of change. It is new sights and sounds. The air smells different in the spring, and nature's touch is lighter.

Spring comes in green: the pale light green of new things growing, and the deep, dark shiny green of fields fortified with fertilizer. In the hills, where grow the fir and spruce and hemlock, the green is of a more somber tone. It looks older, weathered, more permanent than the new-growing greens of the meadow and the valleys.

Spring is the good feel of the sun-warmed earth, and the way it shines in long straight rows behind the plow that rolls it over. Soft, ruffling breezes blow and big whipped-cream clouds drift without hurry across a sea-blue sky. The sun shines brighter then, and stays longer, and no longer glares with winter's cold indifference.

Spring is strong damp odors and oily splotches floating blue and strangely iridescent on puddles of trapped water that never had a chance to run. It is polliwogs wriggling like dark, plump plums in their pools, and the earth still spongy with dampness, and the spear of swamp grass along the ditches.

A meadowlark's song in the pasture is answered by the impudent crow of the pheasant, flaunting his feathery rainbow in the sun near the thicket beside the fence. Spring is a killdeer dragging along the ground, trying to draw the intruder from its nest by faking a broken wing. It is a snipe bursting like a tiny explosion into flight and the zig-zag pattern it flies to safety.

Spring is the time of those soft velvety nights, those dark, star-jeweled hazy moonlit mysteries that shimmer with a suspended, breathless quality, and a sense that some great invisible force awaits the coming of the sun, just waits, as the frogs croak away the stillness and a meteor streaks to a flaming end out there somewhere in the vast reaches of silent space.

Then comes the sun and dark shadows in the peace of early morning. The dew sparkles and spider webs stitched along the fence look fresh as laundered doilies. Birds chitter softly in the deep night-cooled silence and flex their wings. And on a morning in the spring there is something sadly comical in the way a robin tugs and pulls until there is no stretch left and the worm snaps from the ground like a broken spring.

Time becomes important in the spring. It is a pulsating, life-fulfilling time. It can be felt. It can be seen, sprouting and swelling. Expanding. Exploding. Later will come the slow slumberous, ripening time of summer,  but it must wait its turn. Spring must come first. The undeniable force of life must be born to bloom and blossom.

Spring is a time of great potency. The earth is fertile then, and all things strive to be reborn. A flower attracts a bee, and with the pollen it carries away another will be fertilized. The seed that autumn's chill wind scattered in November now finds the strength to sprout and grow.

There is something willy-nilly in the way nature does her thing, but it works. Hers is the grandest plan of all. And there is no equal to the show she puts on in the spring.

# The Joy of October

It comes slowly, gradually, like a tide that's been out for nine long months, to lap gently at September's tattered skirts. And with long, quiet days of great stillness that ripple gently across the face of time it becomes October.

It's the chill of frost glistening in the early morning sun that hesitates on the bleak line of the horizon like a stranger stopped before a forbidden door, a stranger whose smile has lost its warmth, a lonely loner loping across a great pale oval of vaulted sky.

And October is:

Apples red, round and ripe as rosy cheeks, hanging from weary, bending overloaded boughs: long tired arms seeking relief from burdens borne too long, humbly reaching down to ladders reaching up to them. Soon it will be cider time, tangy, tart and tasty. So drink up — old November is coming closer.

Ah yes, October!

A blazing riot of colors, fire flashes that should burn forever: bright, light yellows, and paler lemon hues: reds, bright and lively as new found flames, growing somber as a dying ember. The world all a-rust in the timeless drift of falling leaves that trace that age-old question upon the mystic vapors of a dreamy afternoon: Why here in June and in October gone? Was that the answer? No, 'twas but a sigh such as a gentle breeze might make.

Listen to leaves that rattle so dryly around your feet. And stop. Maybe you'll hear an acorn fall. But listen closely because the sly old oak sows with care. It doesn't want the wily squirrel to know

135

where it's going to begin again. Sly old oak that never talks, that never tells.

And watch the sad old maple broadcast its seed in tiny, two-winged travelers that spin as they descend like crippled choppers whirling to a crash, victims of Nature's desire to see things survive.

October, oozing by like maple syrup, ends the cycle that spring began. All things so carefully planted then — so tenderly tended since spring — have cloned themselves ten times over, every one a miracle that will try next year to do the same: small life capsules stored in golden pumpkin seeds — or lying dormant in the long dark tunnel of a green zucchini hiding beneath an awning of wilted leaves.

Great October, no merry month of May: springtime green turned sere and drear, and the far-off, steely spang of an axe brings down the tree. It's in the air: the rich, thick smell of burning wood, and a lazy ribbon of smoke unwinds a fluffy, white design upon an easel of high blue sky.

October, time of tawny phantoms in the woods: deer, fat and fleshy, slipping into winter just ahead of the hunter's gun. And the lonesome call of geese high on the wing, flying wedges pointed south, sunshine seekers serenely soaring. And sparrows with ruffled wings strung like beads upon the wire, wistful waifs that missed the train.

Then old October frowns, breathes the chill of winter just around the corner, and red and yellow, golden leaves scurry like canaries with broken wings across some deserted road, and flurry among the weeds that stalk in ditches.

Who is this old October that slipped so quietly upon September? What uncanny magic does she work?

Was that the answer?

No, it was hoarse November speaking with a cold.

And October has slipped away, a wise old month is she, that never spends a winter.

# Of Thanksgiving, Things Past

It wasn't much of a road. On a map in some musty, dusty drawer it probably looked like a nice straight thoroughfare. But maps never quite reflect reality. They always manage to hide the ragged edges.

Maybe it wasn't real anyway. Looking back it doesn't seem so. It's more like a chapter from some book read long ago, one that has grown hazy in time and distance. But that's an illusion. The old road was real enough.

It wasn't black-topped then. And cars didn't whiz over it as they do now. But the weather on that particular Thanksgiving Day was the same as it usually is in Oregon during late November.

It was raining, and the road was a mess. It had never been gravelled. It was okay for cars in summer, but in winter it wouldn't tolerate them. With bog holes big as canyons it laid in wait.

We were going to grandma and grandpa's for dinner that day. It wasn't far — a couple of miles at most. But it was quite an undertaking because we had to travel that road. It was the only one that went there.

As we harnessed a team I decided a covered wagon was what we needed. As we led the horses out of the barn a line of them passed slowly through my imagination, each one a warm, snug rolling home on wheels. The rain seemed colder, more dismal and depressing after they had trundled out of sight.

After we had hitched the horses to the old lumber wagon, they stood with drooping heads. The rain splattered their backs and ran down their sides in jerky little streams. What did they have to be thankful for, I wondered, as I huddled up in my coat? And what was I to be thankful for — standing chilled and shivery in the wind?

Across the middle of the wagon we rigged a shelter with a piece of canvas. That's where the food mother had prepared as our share

137

of the dinner would ride. But the dog had other plans. When we got ready to load we found Laddie curled up under the canvas.

As he slunk off toward the porch we quickly shoved everything under the shelter because it was raining hard. We were lucky, mother said, that there were cracks in the bottom of the wagon bed so the water could run out.

Then we crawled aboard: mother and dad, my brother and sister and I. When dad flicked the reins the horses started down the hill. The road that went straight ahead was gravelled. It was smooth and wide. It looked mighty inviting as we turned right.

It wasn't a rough, jolting ride as it would have been on a hard, rutted road. It was more like being adrift on a sea of abrupt heaves. We rocked and rolled and lurched along, and soon the wagon wheels were thick with mud. So were the horses' hooves. When they pulled them out of the thick, gluey gumbo they made a slippery sucking sound.

We had gone about halfway when we passed a small clump of oak trees that grew in the pasture beside the road. In the summer it was a beautiful, park-like place: always cool and shady, always quiet, always still. But it was hard to imagine its beauty as the trees beseeched a low grey sky with stark and leafless limbs.

Grandma and grandpa were pretty well isolated. A drainage ditch that ran in front of their house formed a lake where ducks congregated when it overflowed in winter.

Since it overflowed most frequently, they had their own private lake about six months each year. But it wasn't bright and blue and happy the way lakes should be. It was dark and flat and sullen because it knew it didn't belong there.

I remember distinctly my mood that day. It was definitely sour. Riding a rough old wagon in the rain was not my idea of a holiday. I wondered why the road hadn't been gravelled. I was plenty mad because it hadn't been.

Recently I read in some travel magazine that hay rides on a dude ranch in California have become a very popular form of recreation. Kids today, it seems, find a ride on a wagon pulled by a team of horses a rare treat. And it is — I guess.

So, when Thursday rolls around, I'm going to be thankful I had so many opportunities to enjoy them firsthand, before they had been defiled by gaiety and good humor. Then I'm going to be thankful that I don't have to enjoy them anymore.

# A Witness
# to the Spirit of Christmas

She didn't know I was watching. If she had been aware I'm sure she would have been embarassed. And she might have been shyly pleased if she had known what I was thinking.

She was in her early teens — a girl becoming a woman, which is another of life's wondrous mysteries. She was slender and her face was small and pale. But her hands were quick and strong, and she steered her wheelchair around the store with the ease that comes from long practice. Under the clean blue jeans she wore, her legs didn't make much of an impression.

I don't know who she was. I saw her that one time only, quite a few years ago just before Christmas. I don't even remember the name of the store. But I remember the way she moved, and the thoughtful way she tilted her head when she rolled to a stop in front of something that interested her. She had poise.

But I recall most vividly the happy eagerness with which she went about her business. She liked what she was doing. The smile that shone on each of the gifts she picked was the Yuletide spirit radiated. Generosity came as naturally to her as the sun comes to the morning.

Because there was a mob of late shoppers in the store, she often had to wait before she could enter a crowded aisle. But she didn't get angry or impatient. She smiled as she rolled back to let others pass. It appeared that waiting was something she had become accustomed to.

I, too, was waiting but not with such friendly patience. It wasn't much in evidence anywhere else either. The other shoppers were

139

sober and serious. They looked hurried and harassed. The curse of Christmas shopping had blinded them to the twinkle of the tinsel.

I didn't intend to follow her, but every time I looked up there she was. Unconsciously it may have been because I recognized in her the true spirit of Christmas. It was something sensed rather than seen. Perhaps it was the aura of unselfishness that hovered over that wheelchair — a genuine willingness to give.

He, who was born 2,000 years ago to Mary, died on the cross to symbolize that spirit many times magnified. The significance He has for all mankind is evidence that such spirit is important. When we stray too far from it, when we disregard it too long, we wind up in trouble. History is full of grim examples. Once a year Christmas rolls around to remind us of that. It tweaks our conscience as we reach out to take the needy hand.

As I watched that slender, crippled girl I thought about that. Nothing had to tweak her conscience. Even though I didn't speak one word to her I know that's true. She was without guile. The light that shone in her eyes was the true light. It wasn't shaded by sense of obligation, that crass attitude that we must buy for someone else because they are buying for us: the old Yuletide game of tit for tat.

By the time she met a small, sharp-faced woman near the long line of clanging cash registers her lap was filled with the things she had picked out. As she held them her eyes danced, and the woman I took to be her mother nodded as she talked. But her mind was elsewhere, and it irritated me that she didn't pay more attention to what her daughter was saying.

Then it occurred to me: that's the way it has always been. Charity, generosity and joy must always overcome indifference. They must shine with a steady brilliance or be snuffed out. If it weren't for witnesses like the girl in the wheelchair to keep them glowing that might happen. They make the rest of us take another look at ourselves. They make charity, generosity and joy important.

I believe the things I thought about that girl are true. If they aren't I don't want to know because I need her. She is an example. She — and others like her — make every Christmas memorable.

# Time Shares its Treasures

It's the big events we remember: the million-dollar fire, a murder that steals the headlines, a mountain that blows its top.

They are the emotional skyscrapers in our lives. They excite awe and wonder, anger and resentment. They are the TNT of life.

But they are exceptions. If they came with regularity we would become jaded and indifferent. Our lives would be diminished.

So we are left with all that time when nothing amazing or awe-inspiring is going on. And that's boredom time, say some, a time of dreary doldrums.

But is it?

I thought so as I glanced back at the year just passed for something really impressive. At first there wasn't much to see: no big erupting, flaming sky-high anything that I could remember. In the search for the TNT I had overlooked the treasures.

I had forgotten about hauling hay in the heat under a sky blue as deep water, and how good a breeze feels when it comes, the coolness of shade, and long dark shadows that stretch ahead of evening like dusty streamers.

And I had forgotten the way buzzards circle slowly in the air like time itself unwinding and the way their shadows hurtle across the ground and startle greydiggers that chitter excitedly as they dive for safety in a hole.

And the wind — the wind I love to listen to — I had overlooked completely, and the way it sighs in the oaks and the lazy swaying way they greet it with their limbs as dark green leaves flutter softly and rustle in the sun.

And I had overlooked the clouds that come in from the coast like big white sails, all puffed up and proud as they steer a graceful course across a friendly sky that never threatens with rocks and shoals.

And the cattle — I hadn't remembered them — and the slow, swinging way they come down through the fields for water in the late afternoon, coming slowly in a single file that reminds me of a camel caravan heading into the mysterious East, with dust hanging over them like a tired, exhausted breath.

And what about hummingbirds that come like whirring projectiles that hang like tiny vibrations in the quiet air of early morning as they drill into long slim tunnels of so many colors that decorate the fuschias.

And I hadn't thought of grass that comes in finest green, like a carpet in the spring, new and fresh and tender — more miraculous than anything a store can sell: a gift we take for granted.

And why did I overlook water that runs quick and shy in ditches, that hides in pools and puddles like memories that want to linger on to escape the summer sun that soon will suck them dry?

And still we find life boring. I wonder why. Don't we realize that time is life, that without it we wouldn't be? I wonder why we don't embrace each day as though tomorrow will never come.

Odd, isn't it, that we so often decide to enjoy time after it is gone. And it goes so quickly — and with it life.

142

# Nighttime Magic

Ah, the nights. What moods they create. They play with our emotions. They endow us with great vision, and cripple us with fear. No day can enflame the imaginations the way they can. They are dark and dusky magicians whose trickery knows no end.

On dark and windless, rainy nights a heaviness in the air wraps itself around us softly, like a blanket that hasn't dried. And the gloom is filled with sadness, as if filled to overflowing with all the troubles in the world. On such nights big splashy tears fall listlessly from the trees and spongy skies fill with remorse. All the world is sad and weepy then.

But such times pass. And when all the tears have fallen, the sky shall clear and it will be nighttime celebration time. And such nights they are — those that come when all the sadness has been washed away.

Fairy lands is what they are, where the imagination can loop in endless fantasy through long, smooth planes of misty moonlight. Nights of laughter and gaiety are they. They incite dreams of grandeur. They stimulate an urge for adventure. They blunt sharp edges that gleam in sunlight, and intoxicate with dreams of conquests that become so easy. They are triumphant nights — nights without defeat — and in a pool of moonlight stands the victory circle that waits on us.

But it's a tease. And dawn's pale light brings it to an end. Soon the sun whets all edges sharp again, and the bold thrust of the conqueror's sword becomes a parry that fails to block reality's return. Nights and what they do to us.

Some are treacherous. They dupe and deceive, confuse and confound. They lead our imaginations on wild forays. They take them down strange paths and excite them with sights that don't exist. Such nights float eerie illusions through trembling seas of starlit insubstantiality. Without the moon to light the way, all is muddled murkiness.

And on those nights, shadowy charades that look real enough to be truth itself torment us. They accost us shyly, the way good con men do, and rob us of our certainty. They grab at us with hands that have no fingers. They threaten us with blows that fall soft as shadows, without a sound. With soundless blows that never fall they bruise our imaginations.

There are no victories on those celestial battlefields. They are strewn with anxiety and apprehension. The conquests we achieved, the triumphs we gloated over on moonlit nights, cower in our imaginations as they create dark and shadowy assailants that never quite define themselves. Ghosts prowl at such vaporish times, when only the imagination sees — and far too clearly.

Then come the cold, hard nights, that glitter and gleam in ethereal light, when the sky seems to lift and time and eternity are revealed in one vast, far-reaching curve that ends out there somewhere in the depths of unplumbed space.

We are made then to look inside ourselves, to ponder the imponderable. Those are nights that make us feel things we cannot see — and see things that can only be seen with feeling.

They are nights of paradox: They hint at things we cannot comprehend and tantalize us with the thought that if we knew enough we might just understand. They take the mind out beyond the mortal reef. Out where a billion years have disappeared it becomes befuddled.

On such nights it should stay at 1ome and wait for those that are less demanding.

Like romantic nights, when the Milky Way gets all dressed up for an ethereal ball in a misty, see-through negligee of starry jewels. When it becomes an astronomical carnival the imagination can relax with visions soft and dreamy, all touched so delicately by the master hand of the Mystery Artist.

Ah, the nights. How dull the days would be without them.

144

# ABOUT THE AUTHOR

*Jerry Easterling came late to the writing game. Although he received a degree in Journalism from the University of Oregon shortly after World War II, he spent the next 20 years doing the things that became fodder for the weekly column he began writing for the Statesman-Journal in 1977.*

*He worked as a logger, a sawmill hand, truck driver, carpenter, plus various other odd and unrelated jobs. But most of the time he was in the auction business, which he calls one of the "wildest businesses you could wind up in."*

*In addition to being an auctioneer, he was also a pitchman. For some time he traveled the five western states selling new merchandise at auction. Since 1970, he's been working for newspapers in Salem, Oregon. He is presently a feature writer and columnist for the Statesman-Journal. He, his wife Jeanne, and their family, live on a small farm in the foothills of the Coast Range Mountains, 32 miles west of Salem.*